GHOSTS

OF THE

GRAND

CANYON

About the Authors

Judy Martinez (Tucson, AZ) has been involved with the paranormal since she was about four years old. She realized early on in her life that she had a unique ability to see and sometimes interact with the spirit world. Throughout her life, Judy has tried to help those who are plagued with the supernatural. In 1997, she graduated from the University of Great Falls with a certificate in law enforcement. Shortly after graduation, she entered the Montana State Law Enforcement Academy where she became a maximum security correctional officer. She is originally from Hawthorne, California, but has lived the last thirty-six years all over the country. She is also the cofounder of a paranormal investigation group with her husband Brian-James.

Brian-James Martinez (Tucson, AZ) is a paranormal investigator who's had several ghostly encounters in his life that made him want to learn more about the paranormal field. He is also a US history buff and loves to travel to abandoned ghost towns.

GHOSTS
OF THE
GRAND
CANYON

BY JUDY AND BRIAN-JAMES MARTINEZ

Llewellyn Publications
Woodbury, Minnesota

First Edition

First Printing, 2019

Cover design by Kevin R. Brown

Editing by Brian R. Erdrich

Interior photographs:

Rim Trail (page 12): Miriam and Ira D. Wallach Division of Art; Prints and Photographs Photography Collection, The New York Public Library.

El Tovar Hotel (page 62): Detroit Publishing Company Photo Collection; Library of Congress Prints and Photograph Division.

Bright Angel Lodge (page 28), Verkamp's (page 142): Library of Congress Prints and Photograph Division.

Hopi House (page 130) courtesy of the authors

Llewellyn Publications is a registered trademark of Llewellyn Worldwide Ltd.

Library of Congress Cataloging-in-Publication Data

Names: Martinez, Judy, author.

  Title: Ghosts of the Grand Canyon : personal encounters that will have you on the edge / by Judy and Brian-James Martinez.

  Description: FIRST EDITION. | Woodbury : Llewellyn Worldwide. Ltd., 2019. | Includes bibliographical references.

  Identifiers: LCCN 2018060957 (print) | LCCN 2019004526 (ebook) | ISBN 9780738759982 (ebook) | ISBN 9780738759449 (alk. paper)

  Subjects: LCSH: Ghosts—Arizona—Grand Canyon. | Haunted places—Arizona—Grand Canyon. | Grand Canyon (Ariz.)—Miscellanea.

  Classification: LCC BF1472.U6 (ebook) | LCC BF1472.U6 M383 2019 (print) | DDC 133.1/2979132—dc23

    LC record available at https://lccn.loc.gov/2018060957

Llewellyn Publications
A Division of Llewellyn Worldwide Ltd.
2143 Wooddale Drive
Woodbury, MN 55125.2989
www.llewellyn.com

Printed in the United States of America

Dedication

This book is dedicated to the memory of Judy's beloved big sister, Brenda Sue Crabtree-Long (1954–1982). I love and miss you every day.

And to the memory of Brian-James's loving and caring grandfather, Faustino Avila Martinez (1931–2017). You will forever be in all of our hearts.

Contents

Acknowledgments

I would like to personally thank my friends and extended family at the Grand Canyon, for without you this book would NEVER have been written.

Special thanks to: Mia Bell, Robert "Shelby" Marshall, Leigh and Jackson Mileur, Lee Drumm, Cathy Romero, John and Becka Harrison, Shaun Harris, Jill Brown, Gayle Solis, Lisa Bennett, Dorothy Westmoreland, Brandi McDonald, Amy Neil, and Kimberly Pingilley-Schmitz.

I would also like to thank all of the guests and tourists who visited the Grand Canyon and shared their personal experiences with my husband Brian-James (BJ) and myself. Your stories are what made this book.

Finally, a very special thank you to Benjamin Mollenhour for always supporting my efforts and pushing me forward in the right direction.

INTRODUCTION

Visiting the Grand Canyon was always a big dream of mine. I was born and raised in Hawthorne, California, however my parents owned quite a few acres of land around Bullhead City in western Arizona back in the late sixties through mid-seventies. A few times a year, my family would excitedly leave the hustle and bustle of the greater Los Angeles area for our quaint little cabin in the desert. Unfortunately, every time my family made plans to travel to the Grand Canyon, an illness would befall a family member and we would always have to cancel the trip. By the mid-seventies, my parents had divorced and the properties in Arizona had to be sold, which broke my heart. My love for the state of Arizona has consumed my entire life. My husband and co-author of this book, Brian-James (BJ for short), is originally from East Los Angeles, but eventually settled in Ontario, California. As a child he visited the Grand Canyon with his mom while they were on a trip to visit family in Albuquerque, New Mexico. It was love at first sight for BJ and the canyon. The two of us would stay up late and have long talks about our desire to eventually relocate ourselves to

Arizona. Finally, in the Spring of 2013, we were fortunate enough to be offered a chance to live and work in Arizona—inside Grand Canyon National Park.

There are a couple of different companies that have exclusive contracts to operate in the park, and my personal employment was with the concessionaire, Xanterra (meaning Beautiful Places). Xanterra was founded in 1876, was originally known as the Fred Harvey Company, and is forty years older than the National Park Service (founded in 1916). They operate under the strict supervision of the National Park Service and run the Historic Lodges as well as restaurants like the elegant El Tovar Dining Room and transportation into the canyon via mule rides to the only lodge at the bottom of the canyon, Phantom Ranch.

During my stay there, I worked the front desks of all the lodges as a guest service agent (GSA), and eventually became a lead, but my official position was inside the rustic and historic Bright Angel Lodge, which I was very much in love with. The wonderful people I was honored to work with became like a second family to me. While working behind the front desk, I was able to meet people from all over the world, including NASA astronauts, foreign dignitaries, and famous actors, authors, and athletes. As a guest service agent, you have a very vital and key role in making the guests and visitors to the park feel welcome.

For many first-time international visitors, a guest service agent can be one of their first experiences with American culture. When you have a good rapport with the guests, sometimes they will feel comfortable enough to share the stories of their vacation adventures with you. Shortly after I began working, I noticed that day in and day out, I would overhear various stories from staff and guests alike about supernatural phenomena that they were encountering while in the main village. Having also seen unexplainable events myself around the village area, I had no choice but to become a strong believer that Grand Canyon National Park was one of the most haunted places in the world.

The Grand Canyon is a place that should be visited at least once in your lifetime. Upon first glance of the canyon, most people's thoughts tend to be that of amazement, bewilderment, and of course, grandeur. Then there are the people that can't come up with the words to even begin to describe their first visual sight of the great abyss. In 1949, a female tourist viewing the canyon for the first time actually fainted at the sight of its raw power and was unfortunate enough to have been standing a little too close to a ledge and tumbled six hundred feet to her immediate death. This is just one of the stories that this enormous canyon bestows on its audience.

The Grand Canyon region was carved five to six million years ago and covers 1.2 million acres of land in Northern Arizona, which happens to include the world's largest ponderosa pine forest. The canyon measures one mile deep and up to eighteen miles wide at its most extreme points, while the length is measured by the flow of the Colorado River, which begins at Lees Ferry (mile 0) and ends at Grand Wash Cliffs (mile 277), running through the dry and barren canyon floor. Erosion, flash floods, frost, landslides, and some very creative designs from the Colorado River created this giant carving (though a character from the 1800s by the name of John Hance, who once lived at the Grand Canyon, claimed that he alone created the Grand Canyon by looking for his lost nickel. You can find this story in chapter 6).

The Colorado River is a soul-devouring monster that has claimed many, many lives, however it is also a blessing for many reasons. It runs in the middle of a very large desert and is the life blood to this arid region for sustaining life for plants and animals that call the canyon home, and for thousands of years it has made it possible for many Native American tribes to survive in this dry, harsh environment. Fun fact: the Colorado River that flows through the bottom of the canyon was many years ago known as the Grand River; this is the actual reason why the canyon was named Grand, after the original name of the river.

The park's North Rim towers in elevation at roughly eight thousand feet, while the South Rim stands slightly less at seven thousand feet. Both rims' temperatures are roughly 20 degrees cooler at any given time than at the base of the canyon. At the rims, visitors can enjoy the beauty of the canyon without having to hike to the bottom and its swelteringly deadly heat. The northern portion of the Grand Canyon has bitterly cold winters with an average of 142 inches of snow every year, which forces the National Park Service to shut down the only road that leads into the Grand Canyon's northerly border (AZ-67). The only lodging facility on the North Rim, Grand Canyon Lodge, is just open from May 15 through October 15 due to its severe and dangerous climate. This lodge also is home to several spectral beings. For many of the park visitors, they are very surprised when they discover that the rims are in forested elevation and not in the dry, barren desert that most people assume is all of Arizona, so they don't come prepared for the proper weather conditions. This human error in judgment has caused quite a few fatalities due to freezing to death.

The National Park Service has estimated that the Grand Canyon receives five million visitors a year, but roughly only 5 percent descend into the depths of the canyon by either hiking, rafting, or riding the mules. Unfortunately, there is no elevator or train that will take you to the bottom at this time, despite what some people may have been told. If you want to truly experience one of the most beautiful places on earth, you are going to have to get a little dusty, dirty, and sweaty and hike down one of the many trails. It's well worth the trek and you don't even have to go all the way down—every step you take, you are greeted with a whole new version of the canyon that people who stay up on the rims will never perceive.

Throughout history there have been many different native tribes living within the canyon walls, fighting over land, food, and scarce, precious water. Then the Spanish conquistadors arrived at the canyon's southern rim in the year 1540, desperately looking for the fabled Seven Cities of Cibola (Berger). They tried to claim everything they saw for themselves and took pleasure in ruthlessly killing anyone who stood in their way. In the 1850s the United States government became the new threat to the Native Americans that had called Arizona and the Grand Canyon home for well over twelve thousand years. The government claimed that all the Native American lands now belonged to the United States and sent the U.S. Calvary to forcefully remove any Native who refused to leave. What was done to the Native American people was what I believe to be one of the most horrible atrocities to occur within North American history. Thousands of Natives were ruthlessly murdered while many others lost all of their family members and tribes. They were humiliated and disgraced. The land in and around the Grand Canyon had now become emotionally charged with tears, anger, hatred, and blood.

By the 1880s, the citizens of the United States began hearing stories about a giant hole in the ground within the Arizona

Territory. (I wonder what extraterrestrial beings must think of the human race for staring at a big hole in the ground going oohhh, aahhh—they're probably filming a show called "Craziest Life Forms in the Galaxy: Earth Edition.") Many people wanted to see for themselves what the big hoopla was all about. They started coming by way of train, stagecoach, horse, buckboard, and eventually automobile. Unfortunately, with the higher volume of tourists flooding the canyon, deaths were bound to increase. It is estimated that an average of twelve people die per year at the Grand Canyon. However, some years there may not be any deaths and other years the death toll could be higher. The park originally did not maintain a list of traumatic deaths that happened in and around the canyon. Accidental falls, suicides, murders, sicknesses, drownings, and airplane crashes are just some of the ways people have perished within the Grand Canyon walls. Taking pictures is one of the biggest ways to meet your maker at the canyon. Some tourists seem to need to get that picture no one else has ever gotten, "I will just step on this little ledge and … " They fall three hundred feet to their deaths. Please be aware of this danger.

The National Park Service has done their best at making the Grand Canyon rims and trails as safe as possible for the tourists. In the early 1930s, after the devastating 1929 stock market crash that sent America into the Great Depression, the president of the United States at the time, Franklin Delano Roosevelt, devised a mass stimulus campaign known as the New Deal to help struggling families get back on their feet and get back to work. The Civilian Conservation Corps was a key workforce that was established with Roosevelt's New Deal that hired many unemployed and struggling men to help maintain our national park systems. The retaining wall on the canyon's rim that was originally built to keep tourists from falling over the edge was now going to be reinforced and made stronger. Lookout points and the most populated tourist areas had metal bars installed for safety. The National Park Service did a great job at trying to keep people from falling over dangerous drop-offs.

Please, every person needs to take responsibility for their own actions. The retaining walls were built to protect you and will only work if you follow the rules. Do not climb over them to see the views from the other side because you will end up on the "other side," so to speak. The walls are there for a reason. Stay safe.

The Grand Canyon region also has a high suicide rate. A lot of unhappy people come to the Grand Canyon to jump off one of the rims to end their lives. The movie *Thelma and Louise* (starring Susan Sarandon and Geena Davis) came out in 1991. If you're not familiar with this movie, it is about two women running from the law and ultimately deciding to commit suicide by driving their car off a cliff into the Grand Canyon. Movies are made for entertainment, but some people don't know where to draw the line between fantasy and reality. After *Thelma and Louise* hit the theaters, the Grand Canyon National Park became a hot spot for copycats to commit suicide by driving their car into the great abyss. The National Park Service has had to spray paint some of the death-mobiles that are crumpled on the canyon's floor to blend in with the natural surroundings.

The Bright Angel, North and South Kaibab, Grandview, and even Hermit Trails look deceptively easy going down, but you eventually have to come back up (unless you think you could swim the Colorado River all the way to Lake Mead). Hiking back up is definitely going to be one of the hardest adventures that any hiker will ever undertake. The Bright Angel Trail is the easiest path for those wanting to venture into the canyon depths. However, if the hiker is out of shape or hasn't been physically active for a while, deadly consequences can and will occur. Heart attacks, dehydration, hyponatremia (caused by drinking too much water and losing too much sodium), and heat strokes happen here almost daily. Also, many hikers start their descent believing they are carrying plenty of water to drink and half way down realize they didn't bring an adequate amount. This mistake happens far too often. Weather also plays a factor in the canyon's untimely deaths. Summer monsoonal storms bring flash flooding, rock slides, deadly lightning strikes, and high winds, while the wintertime brings deep snow and frigid temperatures.

The Grand Canyon by itself is truly magical. Just walk to the rim when no one is around (summer months can be a little difficult) and listen to the birds singing and the wind blowing through the trees and bushes. Listen carefully. Did you maybe hear something else? Maybe a human voice behind you calling out your name when there is no one there that you can see? Perhaps you distinctly felt someone place a hand on your back and all of a sudden you were forcefully pushed forward? Maybe you felt something tugging on your hair? The only problem is that you are all alone … or are you? There are many reports of people hearing unexplained sounds and seeing unexplainable things all throughout the canyon and surrounding areas. I lived at the Grand Canyon and I can tell you that you're not imagining things. Tourists and locals have claimed to have seen UFOs flying all around the canyon depths. Guests staying at the hotels have claimed to have been attacked by ghosts. The Pioneer Cemetery near Market Plaza is a peaceful experience until you witness a dark shadow peering out at you from behind a tree and you walk over to the tree to see who it is and no one is there.

Upon the deaths of some individuals around the canyon, their spirits have decided they just want to hang around the canyon, lodges, and trails. Who can blame them? It is the Grand Canyon after all. Some ghosts here just seem to be happy for their eternal views and then there seems to be a few spirits that are malicious and have some anger management issues. So let me take you to the land of ghosts and hauntings of the Grand Canyon Village. Hopefully you will be able to make it out alive. If you don't, it's OK, at least you read this book. Hey, look at this way—you will be adding to the ghostly lore of the canyon.

Chapter 1
THE RIM TRAIL

The Grand Canyon's Rim Trail is a thirteen-mile, one-way, relatively easy hiking trail and a fantastic way to see the canyon first-hand from the top of the South Rim. You can begin the journey at Hermit's Rest and head east. You will walk through forested areas with ponderosa pine, pinion, and juniper trees to your right, to the beautiful abyss of the Grand Canyon to your left. Most of the trail is paved but be warned: there are areas where it is simply dirt and rocks with just a few pine tree needles sprinkled on top for color and there are areas with uneven stairs. At Pima Point you will be able to see the Colorado River and, if you're lucky, an eagle-eye view of one of the water rafting trips floating by. In this area, if it is quiet enough, you can faintly hear the roar of the Colorado River going over the Lava Falls Rapids echoing up through the canyon walls.

While walking the trail, you will pass by Monument Creek Vista, Mojave Point, Hopi Point, Powell Memorial (supposedly the first man to successfully navigate the Colorado River inside the Grand Canyon), and Maricopa Point. As you continue heading east, you will eventually pass by the outdoor Sunday morning worship site. Located in this area are the two graves of husband and wife

Charles and Olga Brandt. Charles was one of the very first managers of the El Tovar Hotel, and both husband and wife decided that they wanted to be buried overlooking the El Tovar Hotel instead of being buried inside the Grand Canyon's Pioneer Cemetery. Mr. and Mrs. Brandt both passed away in the early 1920s. A beautiful spot near the Sunday morning worship site off the beaten path of the Rim Trail was chosen for their eternal resting place. The Brandts had a prized Airedale dog named Razzle Dazzle who was adopted and well cared for by a resident of the Grand Canyon Village upon their deaths. After the dog died in 1928, Razzle Dazzle was interred with the Brandts at their burial site. These graves are difficult to find if you don't know where to look; it is possible that there could be other people throughout history buried near the canyon's rim.

A vintage postcard of the Grand Canyon's Rim Trail

Not much farther down the trail, hikers will enter into the historic Grand Canyon Village. The park lodges offer free water for your canteens as well as restrooms, gift stores, and restaurants. Outside the Bright Angel Lodge is the famed Soda Fountain where you can purchase a variety of delicious ice cream. My husband was known to frequent this location as I worked behind this lodge's front desk. He was not allowed to visit me unless he had bought me a chocolate shake. After you get your ice cream, take a short walk to the rim and keep a watchful lookout for the majestic California condors soaring on the thermal winds emanating from the canyon's floor. These massive birds have built their nests into the canyon walls' crevices.

Continue trekking east and you will come across a marker that lets you know that you have arrived at the Trail of Time. It is a self-guided geological walking tour where you will see actual geologic samples taken from the numerous rock layers that make up the Grand Canyon. In just one and a half miles, you will see and experience millions of years of geologic history. At the end of the Trail of Time is the Yavapai Geology Center, where you can learn how the canyon was formed. Once you are done visiting the Yavapai Geology Center, continue on your walk and you will pass the park's main visitor's center, which includes Mather Point and eventually end your hike at Organ Pipe Vista.

During this hike, you will have seen incredible vistas, plateaus and the bridge that crosses the Colorado River to Phantom Ranch. (Phantom Ranch hauntings are not included inside this book. It was named "Phantom" because it is hidden from most views from the rims as well as inside the canyon itself). The views are stunning and will take your breath away. You may have passed on your journey an abundance of wildlife such as elk, deer, mountain rams, rabbits, raccoons, and squirrels. You have also just walked by where many people have fallen to their deaths looking at this canyon in the same spots you were.

Many people have fallen accidentally, while others have purposely thrown themselves into the dark reaches of the abyss hoping their souls would finally find peace. There have also, sadly, been many deaths from people taking pictures too close to unstable rocks and soft soil. Likewise, there have been senseless deaths due to people going rock climbing and jumping from rock to rock on the rims. Then you have the preoccupied people who just aren't paying attention to that next step in front of them. It's a sheer cliff on the other side of that trail and there's not much to break your fall. Only a very few lucky people have survived falling from the rim, but these people have suffered life-altering injuries. With that said, for those who truly love true ghost stories, the Rim Trail has given us a bottomless array of paranormal activity. All anyone has to do is walk in any direction, have an open mind, and wait. Sometimes you don't have to wait long and sometimes you don't even have to be a believer in the paranormal, but the canyon can and will make a true skeptic run for their life.

The Wicked Within

Tara was a very excited young woman, having just two weeks prior been hired as a guest service agent (front desk) at the historic Bright Angel Lodge. She found out not long after relocating to the park that her longtime boyfriend, who was now her fiancé, was also set to be hired to work inside the park. He wouldn't be there for another three weeks, however, so they couldn't start their new lives working and living together at the Grand Canyon just yet. Officially employed at the park now, Tara was assigned to be housed in the old and rustic yet historic Colter Hall, a female-only dormitory for single employees. Colter Hall is situated directly next to the world-famous El Tovar and Kachina Lodges, features a long-abandoned secret hidden tunnel where the young Harvey

Girls would walk to and from work at the El Tovar (as not to disturb any visitors) and is just a very short walk to the Rim Trail. One day, right after Tara got off work, she went back to her room to retrieve a letter that she had written for her fiancé the night before. She decided to go to the El Tovar lobby to mail off her letter, as the local post office was around two miles away and she didn't have her own transportation. This was in late March of 2013 and the weather was still quite chilly outside for that time of year. Although Tara loved her fiancé, she wasn't about to freeze her butt off for a letter. Little did Tara know that this simple act of convenience nearly turned tragic.

Tara was absolutely ecstatic about seeing her fiancé soon, so nothing else of importance was on her mind. She dropped the letter into the El Tovar's mail box and exited the building through the lobby's front doors. Tara decided that she wanted to go towards the Rim Trail then immediately noticed that there really weren't many tourist swarming towards the rim to watch the multicolored sunset, which only the canyon can offer. It had been a chilly day, and as the sun came closer to setting, it was obvious it was going to be a brutally cold night—but that doesn't usually stop the visitors from watching the sun go down. With no one else around, Tara was casually walking west on the trail when a feeling of immense depression consumed her. She felt like she was going to cry … but why? When Tara reached an area on the trail near the Arizona Room Restaurant, where there was no retaining wall, she heard a woman's voice deliberately, directly, and forcefully whisper in her ear, "Go to the rim and jump." Tara swiftly turned around to see who would say such an awful thing to a stranger.

To her unsettling amazement, there was no one there, not a single tourist or employee. She was all alone. More than a little startled, she thought she must have imagined it. As Tara approached the canyon's rim, once again she heard a distressed woman's voice demanding her to "JUMP." The disembodied voice sounded angrier and more agitated than before. Surveying her surroundings, she could see that no living being was anywhere in sight. Saying Tara was scared doesn't even begin to explain the fear and dread she was sensing or the thought that something she couldn't see was going to try to harm her. Tara was 100 percent positive that she heard the woman's voice in her ear telling her to jump. Frozen in fear for what must have seemed like an eternity, she finally summoned up the courage to get away from the rim as quickly as she possibly could. She eventually got back to the safety of Colter Hall not long after her ordeal. The sun could never set again as far as she was concerned. It simply wasn't worth it for her.

Tara had only been employed at the Grand Canyon for two weeks. She didn't know anyone well enough to tell them about what she had just experienced. When she was safely in her room at Colter Hall, she sat and asked herself if she really did hear a ghost or demon tell her to go to the rim and jump. She wanted to know if anyone else had ever experienced this evil voice trying to get people to jump into the canyon, but who could she talk to who wouldn't think she was crazy? A week after Tara had her strange experience of the voice telling her to jump off the rim, she overheard some fellow coworkers discussing ghosts stories about the Grand Canyon Village. Tara pulled Lisa, one of the employees, aside, feeling comfortable enough to confide in her about the experience. When Tara told Lisa what had happened to her a week earlier, Lisa had this look of dread on her face.

"Oh my god, that happened to you too?" Lisa asked Tara. Lisa, herself, was finally able to tell someone about her experience with a similar disembodied voice on the Rim Trail.

A few months before Tara had been hired, Lisa and a friend were walking on the trail behind the Hermit's Rest bus transfer. It was around sunset, and as Lisa and her friend were approaching the head of the Bright Angel Trail, a woman's voice said sternly into Lisa's ear to go to the rim and jump, yet Lisa's friend never heard a thing. Again the voice, angrier this time, demanded that Lisa go to the rim and jump. Lisa said that after the second time the voice told her to jump, an overwhelming feeling of sorrow enveloped her and she wanted to jump into the canyon. Lisa's friend noticed she was acting strangely and took her away from that area and the depressed feeling dissipated. Lisa to this day will not go near the Rim Trail.

A day after Tara and Lisa confided in each other, Laura, another employee, came forward and stated that she also was told by a female voice behind the Bright Angel Lodge to kill herself and that her life was pointless. Laura also was walking with a friend who did not hear the voice. A feeling of despair had consumed Laura, but this time the ghost became physical. After she heard the voice and became depressed, she felt someone or something *push* her on her back towards the rim. Shocked, Laura turned away from the rim to run when she was forcefully shoved towards a cliff 250 feet above the canyon. Laura was terrified that something she couldn't even see was trying to kill her. Laura's friend was watching what Laura was going through, but she claimed that something immobilized her and she was unable to move. Laura was finally able to escape the ghost's physical attack and has refused to go near any of the canyon's rims for any reason.

Stay Forever

Is there a ghost hanging around the Rim Trail waiting to ambush unsuspecting tourists and employees? Take Bridget, who came to the Grand Canyon for the first time in July with her husband and a couple of friends. Their plan was to be in Monument Valley later that night, so they decided to make a quick stop for a few hours at the Grand Canyon. Bridget and her best friend Robyn decided to hike down the Bright Angel Trail to the three-mile rest house while their husbands hung around on the rim waiting to see the California condors. The trail was crowded with teenagers and small children running around with no parental supervision. The two friends decided it just wasn't safe to hike so they chose to turn around at the one-and-a-half-mile rest house and come back up. When they almost reached the top of the trail, they noticed they were finally alone. No one was coming up or down the trail at that moment. Now they could enjoy themselves for a little while and take in the view. They were at the last tunnel before reaching the top of the trail head and decided to hang out there. They had heard about ancient Native American petroglyphs around the tunnel and started looking for them, enjoying the solitude. They regretted not being able to stay longer at the canyon, but they were on a time limit and they had to depart soon for Monument Valley.

As the two ladies started slowly hiking back up to the top, Bridget distinctly heard a female voice next to her say "Jump." She turned and looked at Robyn, who had stopped on the trail a few feet behind her, taking pictures of a flower that was growing out of a cactus. Bridget figured she must have heard someone's voice echoing from inside the canyon. As the two friends continued their journey to the top, once again Bridget heard the same female voice, but this time it said, "You have to jump." Bridget turned to Robyn and asked her if she just told her to jump. Robyn jokingly asked her why she would ask her to jump when she could just push her into the canyon if she wanted too. But then Bridget said,

"If you didn't say it, then who did?" Robyn suggested that the heat must be getting to her because she never heard a woman's voice telling anyone to jump.

After the two friends reached the top of the Bright Angel Trail, they decided to go into the Bright Angel Lounge to relax and get a well-deserved drink. At the front desk, Tara and Lisa were catching up on their daily paperwork. Bridget left the lounge to use the woman's restroom located down the hall from the front desk. Still puzzled about her weird experience on the trail, Bridget figured it couldn't hurt to stop by the front desk and ask if anyone else had ever reported hearing disembodied voices around the Bright Angel Trail. As Bridget approached the desk, Tara was concentrating on her work but glanced and gave a friendly "Hi. How can I help you?" Bridget asked if she could ask her a stupid question. Tara silently prepared herself for the mother of all stupid questions. Smiling, Tara said, "Sure, ask away."

Bridget seemed embarrassed at first but then quickly asked if Tara knew if the Grand Canyon was haunted in any way. This kind of question was not what Tara was expecting to hear but was intrigued to find out if this visitor was looking for a haunted location or if something otherworldly had happened to her. Curious, Tara asked her what she meant by haunted. After a minute she let out the whole story about what she experienced on the trail, with the woman's voice telling her to jump multiple times but her friend Robyn claiming she never heard a thing. Tara was thrilled with what she was hearing and loudly exclaimed with excitement, "I have heard the same voice and so have many other people."

Bridget, now ecstatic that someone believed her, excused herself to go and retrieve her friend from the lounge. Tara quickly called Lisa over as soon as Bridget and Robyn showed up. The front desk staff assured Bridget that she was not alone in hearing a disembodied voice telling her to jump, and if you're with a group of people, most times only one person will hear the voice. Bridget thanked Tara and Lisa and said they were late meeting their husbands to finish their trip to Monument Valley. If Bridget only knew that she was one of the luckier victims of this evil ghost.

Come to the Other Side

Ashley resides in Flagstaff, Arizona, which is roughly eighty-one miles one way to the Grand Canyon. She made her weekly trip to the canyon to see her on-again, off-again boyfriend who was working for the park service. Having a boyfriend that worked at the Grand Canyon was her pot of gold at the end of the rainbow, because she loved nothing more than to be at the canyon. It was in March of 2014, and Ashley would have her most terrifying experience she had ever encountered in her entire life—and it was all complimentary, thanks to the haunted Grand Canyon's Rim Trail. On this one particular day in March, Ashley was lazily walking the Rim Trail heading west after parking her car in the El Tovar/Hopi House parking lot. Her destination was to go on the Rim Trail behind the Bright Angel Lodge's historic Rim Cabins and next to the Lookout Studio so she could find a quiet place to sit on the ground with her back against the retaining wall.

Ashley was an aspiring artist and loved to draw sketches of the historic buildings that make up the Grand Canyon Village. (If you ever walk any part of the Rim Trail, you quite possibly could encounter many artist drawings or painted landscape scenes from different parts of the canyon.) Within this area where Ashley chose to sit, she wasn't in anyone's way, and this was also one of her favorite places to normally sit and wait to meet up with her boyfriend. The sun was out with a few clouds blowing by and a slight cool breeze. As she sat back against the rocks that made the retaining wall, she thought she heard something moving around on the other side of the barrier. She knew that was impossible because it was a sheer cliff and almost nothing to break a person's fall except a little bit of shrubbery. She figured it must be one of those annoying squirrels that frequent the walls looking for a bird-brained tourist who will give them a handout. As she sat back and tried to get comfortable, Ashley felt hands wrap around her throat from behind and the grip instantaneously cut off her breathing. She tried to grab for her assailant's hands that had seized her neck and realized she was grabbing at nothing but air and her own throat. She couldn't scream and then tried to squirm out of the deadly grip to no avail.

Ashley could now feel that her ghostly assailant was trying to pull her up and over the retaining wall. This murderous entity was physically able to lift her up about six inches off the ground before it finally released its deadly hold. As soon as Ashley realized the threat was gone she became distressed and sobbed uncontrollable. When she was able to gain composure she quickly grabbed her belongings and ran for safety. When Ashley explained to her boyfriend about what she went through, he tried his best to comfort her but didn't seem too surprised upon hearing about her experience. Quite a few of the park employees have heard stories about strange occurrences that have happened in and around the canyon. There is also a belief by many people that the canyon calls to them. Victims have claimed this summoning draws them against their will to the canyon's rim as if in a trance. Once there, they are overcome with a feeling to leap into the huge cavity within the earth known as Grand Canyon.

Gone Too Soon

As I previously mentioned, many different types of people throughout history have died suddenly and tragically within the confines of the southern rim, either by accident or by choice.

I have extensively searched many books and history records and I think I might know who this vengeful spirit could possibly be. Jennifer was a twenty-eight-year-old woman who had been working in the park for almost a year. Although she would smile at all the park's daily visitors, Jennifer's personal life was falling apart and a friend of hers had conveyed to me that this once fun and playful girl that he knew and loved had seemingly become a completely different person overnight. She began drinking heavily and could become confrontational in a blink of an eye. Jennifer had been given some devastating news about a court case involving a family member. Her whole life came crashing down around her and she went to the Bright Angel Lounge to drown her sorrows. After a while of intense drinking, Jennifer became even more upset when the bartender refused to serve her any more alcoholic drinks.

It was about 12:30 a.m. when Jennifer left the bar and proceeded out the Bright Angel Lodge's back doors towards the dark rim. Bright Angel Lodge's front desk employee Luke followed the intoxicated woman and watched her climb up on the retaining wall. He told her to get down, and the distraught and inebriated woman said she was going climbing.

Luke then ran into the Bright Angel Lodge and called the park's dispatch for help. By the time the park rangers arrived, Jennifer was already in serious trouble. She had fallen off the wall and slid down the steep slope towards a cliff. She was screaming and begging for someone to save her. The rangers had a hard time locating her because it was pitch black outside. Even their flashlights were of little use. The rangers were trying their best to form a rescue team. Her cries and screams were piercing the night air and the rangers tried very hard to calm her fears. Every couple of minutes she would slide farther down the steep slope closer towards the deep chasm. Jennifer was desperately holding on to small brush, rocks, and anything else she could to keep her from sliding farther towards the sheer drop off.

It was now a little after 1:00 a.m. and the rangers were starting to lose hope. They had tried to throw Jennifer a rope to grab so they could pull her up, but she was so terrified to let go that she wouldn't dare reach out for the life line. After a little over a half hour of fighting for her life, Jennifer's strength finally gave out and she slipped off the cliff and all the frantic rangers' hearts stopped when they heard terrified and gut-wrenching screams as she plummeted to her death inside the canyon walls.

I believe it could be possible that when Jennifer walked out to the rim that night that she could have been considering suicide. She had been very depressed and upset with the way things were going in her personal life. Nobody had actually witnessed her fall off the retaining wall but I think after she tumbled down the slope she realized that committing suicide was not the answer and tried any way she could from falling to her death, but the canyon had already heard her cries and accepted her as its own. What happened to Jennifer became a living nightmare. Her life had become a mess, and whether her fall from the retaining wall was an accident or intentional, it will forever remain a mystery. What is known is that there had been no recorded paranormal activity around this area until after Jennifer's untimely death. It's possible that her spirit wants revenge for not having the life she thought she deserved, or because the rangers who were trying desperately to save her life were not successful and she wants vengeance on anyone enjoying life who crosses her path.

Legends of the Fall

There is a ghostly legend about a Civilian Conservation Corps (CCC) member who was helping to build the safety railing around Maricopa Point lookout, where he supposedly fell to his death in the 1930s or 1940s. Witnesses have claimed that they have seen a black shadow person lurking around this lookout. Upon my research, I could not find any documents to confirm that any CCC employee fell to his death at Maricopa Point. On the other hand, there are documented reports of several people having committed suicide by jumping off the steep, jagged cliffs at this spectacular point and into the depths below.

Don't Look Back

Many canyon dwellers like to find a quiet, solitary, and peaceful area that overlooks the canyon views to sit, relax, and for some new-agers, meditate. Park employees endure long days dealing with guests and visitors by checking them into their rooms and trying to assist angry overnight guests on where they can find parking inside the village area, especially at the Bright Angel Lodge. Everyone has their own unique method of relieving stress after a hard and strenuous day of work. Some find going home and watching television helps, while others (like my husband) live for playing video games. Still other people prefer to go to a local bar and have a few drinks, while a few like to go to the gym and literally exercise the stress away. Park employee Jessica loved to meditate at the end of her day and she even had her own special hiding place east of the El Tovar Hotel, just before the Trail of Time begins. One evening before the sun set, Jessica decided to walk to her special "sanctuary." She placed a blanket on the ground, then sat down, crossed her legs, took in a long breath, and closed her eyes like she's always done before.

Jessica enjoyed the peace and quiet for roughly ten minutes before she heard something rustling around behind her. Thinking it was one of the park's many elk, she tried to tune out the noise that was interfering with her zen time. Only a few minutes later, Jessica clearly heard footsteps walking right up behind her. As she turned her head to see who or what it was, no one was there. Convinced that she was alone, Jessica turned her head back towards the canyon and reclosed her eyes. Within seconds, Jessica was hit with an overpowering feeling of dread and despair. The hair on the back of her neck and arms stood straight up, with chills enveloping her whole body. She could sense someone or something watching her every move. Had she become prey for something that wanted to harm her? The thought of it being a cougar had briefly crossed her mind, but they are very rarely seen near the main village.

Firmly believing she was in imminent danger, Jessica jumped up as fast as she possibly could to confront whatever it was she was feeling threatened by, but realized she didn't have anything to protect herself with. To her relief, she didn't see anyone in her vicinity. But even though she couldn't visibly see anything, Jessica's gut instinct still told her that something wasn't right. She grabbed her blanket and started making her way back towards the Rim Trail, where she hoped there would be safety in numbers. Then, without warning, Jessica came face to face with a pitch-black shadow person standing right in front of her, blocking her path.

Even though she was terrified, she could clearly make out that the shadow had a human form but was obviously not human at all. As she stood looking at it, trying to figure out what it was, it quickly faded away right in front her eyes. Jessica bolted towards the trail as fast as her legs could carry her. By now, Jessica's heart was pounding and she felt weak in her knees. When she reached the Rim Trail, she noticed no one else walking around. Jessica started heading west towards the El Tovar Hotel, then she stopped and turned around to see if she was finally safe and sound. To her dismay, she now witnessed several other shadow beings dodging behind trees and rocks like they were playing hide and seek with her—but Jessica was not in a playing mood.

Most of the shadows were only about three feet tall with a general human shape. She was able to make out that the shadows had humanlike legs and arms. Jessica was beyond petrified and started to run again as fast as she could back to the El Tovar Hotel. She knew she had a friend who was working inside the gift shop that night. Jessica broke down and started to cry uncontrollably. She told her friend about the horrifying experience that just occurred. Her friend was getting off work soon, so she hung around inside the El Tovar lobby to avoid having to walk alone to Colter Hall, where she resided. Jessica decided that life in Grand Canyon Village wasn't for her. Shortly after this harrowing experience, Jessica left the park permanently for ghost-free pastures elsewhere.

The Grand Canyon's Rim Trail offers some of the most beautiful and spectacular views for anyone to behold. Everyone should see the Grand Canyon at least once in their lifetime. Just remember, in two words, "Stay Safe," or you just might become one of the many ghosts that call Grand Canyon home.

Chapter 2
BRIGHT ANGEL LODGE

The name "Bright Angel" originated from famed Grand Canyon explorer John Wesley Powell. Powell was born in 1834, in Mount Morris, New York. As a young child, John's family was financially unstable. His father was a traveling preacher and struggled to support his wife and children. Unfortunately for young John and his siblings, moving from town to town was a necessity so that his father could preach the good book and feed his growing family from donations he received through his congregations. When John Powell came of age, he enlisted in the Civil War for the "Yankees," officially known as the Union. Within two months after enlisting, Powell was promoted to lieutenant. During the battle of Shiloh, he was shot in his right arm and the field surgeons were unable to save the appendage. Powell did not let the amputated limb destroy his life and refused to sit back quietly and watch the world go by as a mere spectator.

After the Civil War ended, Powell decided he wanted to organize an expedition to explore the Colorado River and the land it flowed through. On May 24,1869, Powell and his team launched four boats from Green River City, Wyoming. The plan was to go down the Green and Colorado Rivers, through the Grand Canyon, and to end the journey at Grand Wash Cliffs near present day Lake Mead. In the beginning of the expedition, everything was going smoothly. Eventually, the explorers ran into white water on the Green River, which resulted in the loss of one of their boats and a third of their limited supplies in a set of backbreaking rapids. On August 4, Powell and his men finally reached the beginning of the Grand Canyon, but the Colorado River flowing through it was anything but welcoming. The rapids were sometimes more than three stories high, and at times there was nothing more than sheer cliffs on both sides of the white water, which would mean certain death to anyone unlucky enough to fall.

The Bright Angel Lodge, circa 1933

The inner canyon's scorching heat was well over 100 degrees Fahrenheit daily and was taking its toll on the crew. Powell and his team must have wondered what kind of hell they had gotten themselves into. On the warm summer evening of August 27, the exhausted explorers were camping next to a riverbank. After a few of the men surveyed the next portion of the river that they would have to challenge the next day, the men soon realized it was going to be the deadliest set of white water rapids they would have ever encountered to date. The majority of the crew had their doubts about making it out of the next day's quest alive.

Three men on the team (Oramel Howland, Seneca Howland, and William H. Dunn) decided that they stood a better chance of survival if they hiked out from the canyon's floor. Powell tried to stop them but the minds of the three men were firmly set. The next morning, the two Howland brothers and Dunn started their difficult trek up the five-thousand-foot canyon walls into the even more dangerous desert terrain in extreme heat towards the North Rim. These three men were never seen or heard from again.

Powell, however, did conduct a search party for them after the completion of his historic trip and was told that the three men met their ultimate fate when they came across Southern Paiute Native Americans on the Arizona Strip, north of the Grand Canyon near Mount Trumbull. I have a weird feeling that these three former crew members' spirits are still hanging around the canyon's North Rim area, angry and probably a little thirsty having realized in their afterlife that they screwed up big time for abandoning their employer, coworkers, and friends.

The remaining explorers in Powell's group fearfully set off the next morning to conquer the most harrowing set of rapids they had ever seen. Fortunately, due to Powell's picking of well-experienced explorers, every man survived and there was very little loss of supplies and equipment. In that day and time, boats were made of pine and oak, and every man had to put all of his strength into keeping the wooden boats from being torn apart from any hazards the Colorado River might have thrown at them. It wasn't until the 1900s that water-tight rafts with motors took over as the way to "safely" travel this deadly river.

During their travel through the canyon's depths, this exhausted and beaten group of men happened to float by a parcel of land that could pass as Utopia to Lt. John Wesley Powell. This piece of land contained a beautifully bewitching creek, winding its way down through a gorgeous red canyon. Near this life-giving stream was a large and inviting tree. The expedition team decided to camp here for a couple of days to rest and to regain their lost energy. John Wesley Powell accordingly named this creek "Bright Angel" because this area was a little piece of heaven inside a malignant chasm. This parcel of land now houses the famed Grand Canyon's Phantom Ranch.

The Bright Angel Lodge and Cabins stand on the site of the old Bright Angel Hotel and Camps. The hotel and camps were built by James Thurber in 1896 close to the Bright Angel trailhead, which lead down into the inner depths of the canyon. Thurber also ran the Bright Angel's Trail, and visitors who wanted to hike down had to pay a one dollar access fee (which would equal twenty-eight dollars today) to gain passage. This hotel and camp site was the first overnight lodging facility within the Grand Canyon Village. In 1901 Thurber sold the Bright Angel Hotel and Camps to Martin Bugguln, whom gave the Atchison, Topeka and Santa Fe Railway (part of the Fred Harvey Company) a partial interest in the hotel and camps. When Bugguln took over ownership, the sleeping tents in the camp were given a desperately needed upgrade with new comfortable beddings, and each tent was issued a heater for the bitterly cold winter nights. After the improvements were completed, these sleeping quarters were now advertised as "Tent-Cabins." Even with the renovations, the new cabins were still cheaper to rent for a night and an alternative to the pricey rooms that the El Tovar Hotel offered.

In 1879, William "Buckey" O'Neill arrived in the Arizona Territory at the tender age of nineteen. His nickname "Buckey" was given to him because he was a notorious gambler and often "bucked the odds" at the card game faro. Following Buckey's arrival in Arizona, he quickly became a major player within the history of the state. He owned his own newspaper, was a lawyer, served as a district court recorder, a probate judge, became superintendent of schools, an advocate in establishing the Atchison, Topeka and Santa Fe Railway going to the Grand Canyon Village, and was a tax assessor. He accomplished all this before the ripe, old age of thirty. Later in life he served as the mayor of Arizona's first territorial capital, Prescott, and became the sheriff of Yavapai County. Being in Arizona, he of course he had to try his hand in mining, which didn't pan out (pun intended). As time went on, Buckey became good friends with the future president of the United States, Theodore Roosevelt, and eventually joined Roosevelt's Rough Riders as a captain. Buckey participated in the Spanish-American War in Cuba, and on July 1, 1898, was shot and killed during the battle at San Juan Hill, the fight that made Teddy Roosevelt's Rough Riders internationally famous. William "Buckey" O'Neill was only thirty-eight years old at the time of his death. Even though he had a busy and short life, Buckey loved nothing more than to be at the canyon and had built a handsome cabin in 1890 next to the Bright Angel Hotel within feet of the rim. This historic cabin still exists to this day and is the oldest standing original structure on the South Rim, simply known as the Buckey Suite.

Another historic building, known as the Red Horse Suite, now sits on the property that houses the Bright Angel Lodge and Cabins. This magnificent rustic building was originally built in 1890 by Ralph Cameron as a ranch house and a stage relay station near Red Horse Wash, which is located thirty-five miles southeast of the Grand Canyon Village. After the building was first constructed, it became a stagecoach stop for all the weary travelers heading towards Grand Canyon. Before the turn of the twentieth century, the Grand Canyon Railroad had not yet been established, however there was a railroad line that had been constructed that linked Chicago to Los Angeles. This westbound railway—as luck would have it—went through Flagstaff and Williams, Arizona. From one of these stops, the tourists who were traveling north to the Grand Canyon would have to finish their journey by renting a horse or purchasing a ticket for a stagecoach. If the traveler departed the train in either of these towns and transferred over to stagecoach to finish the remainder of the journey towards the Grand Canyon, this meant they could expect horrible weather conditions including oppressive heat and intense monsoonal storms during the summer months.

Those foolhardy enough to travel to Northern Arizona during the winter season (which can feel like an eternity) experienced severe snow storms, deep snow drifts, and bitterly cold temperatures that can dip below freezing for weeks at a time. Traveling before the invention of the automobile could have been deadly because of the outside elements, but to add insult to injury, the dirt roads weren't maintained so the wagon trails were either muddy and rutty or dusty and dry and it could have taken days to weeks to have arrived at their final destination. The stagecoaches' last stop before reaching the canyon was at the Red Horse Station. Here the passengers could get out of the stagecoach, stretch their legs, and get something to eat and drink, while the horses were attended to or switched out for fresher ones if needed. Some passengers didn't realize that the canyon was located in a very remote and isolated area in the Northern region of Arizona, which made for horribly grumpy travel companions (warning—this still happens today, even with the invention of the automobile).

At the turn of the century, the automobile was quickly becoming the most popular way to travel. Stagecoach stops were quickly becoming a thing of the past, so the people who ran them had to find a new way to make a living, and more often than not that required having to move elsewhere. Most of these old wooden structures were abandoned to rot and wither away with the elements. In 1902, Ralph Cameron wasn't about to let go of his livelihood or the building he loved, and decided to relocate the Red Horse Station (log by log) to its present day location and turn it into a two-story hotel. After the Red Horse Station had been completely reassembled, it was renamed the Cameron Hotel. It also served as the Grand Canyon post office for a short time, until a new building was constructed in 1935. Later that same year, the Bright Angel Hotel underwent a major remodel and the National Park Service had planned to demolish the Red Horse Station/Cameron Hotel. Architect Mary Elizabeth Colter was able to save this aging, historic building. The once two-story Cameron Hotel was renovated, and the second floor was disassembled. The cabin was also given a new name now known as the Red Horse Suite. This is my favorite building in the whole park. If you are able, treat yourself for a night in this historical cabin. It's worth it, even though at this time no hauntings have been reported within it.

In the 1920s, the Fred Harvey Company asked famed female architect Mary Elizabeth Colter if she could design a new facility to eventually replace the aging Bright Angel Hotel and tent-cabins. In her designs, she was able to save Buckey O' Neill's cabin and the Cameron Hotel from demolition due to their historical values. In 1935, the new lodge and cabins had been completely renovated to resemble a pioneer settlement. Inside the Bright Angel Lodge is the registration desk, transportation desk (where you can book mule rides, overnight stays at Phantom Ranch, and sightseeing tours), the Bright Angel Restaurant, and the most popular gift shop within all of the national parks. This lodge also offers water bottle-filling station, restrooms, a coffee bar/lounge that offers live entertainment during the summer months, and a history museum that offers tourists a glance at the Harvey Girls' uniforms, an 1800s buggy, and the legendary stone fireplace that Mary Colter designed to reproduce the strata found in the Grand Canyon in their correct sequences, from top to bottom. This lodge also has in its possession an antique wooden rocking horse made in the 1890s for a child of one of the first families to have resided on the canyon's rim. The lodge also has a large fireplace in the lobby for the cold soul in the winter-time. Outside the lodge on the north side is the ice cream shop known simply as The Fountain. On the east side of Bright Angel Lodge is the famous Arizona Room Restaurant. This dining room offers some of the best steaks in the entire state of Arizona. The Bright Angel Lodge and Cabins has a little bit of something to keep all of its visitors entertained.

During the renovation, Mary Colter designed multiple sleeping quarters inside the new Buckey Lodge that was designed around Buckey O'Neill's historic cabin. The Powell Lodge, named after famed explorer John Wesley Powell, was built adjacent to the Buckey Lodge and it also has multiple sleeping quarters. Both of these lodges have simple rooms known as Hiker's Specials. There are no televisions sets within these rooms, and the majority of these rooms do not come equipped with bathrooms. There are shared showers and restrooms that can be accessed through a door within the lodge's inner hallways. These are the cheapest rooms in the park for visitors on a budget. Buckey O'Neill's actual historic cabin can be rented nightly. It is a beautiful cabin and can sleep up to five adults. There is a historical sign out in front of the Buckey O'Neill Suite on the rim side. Please be aware that this cabin is NOT a museum. You may look at it from the Rim Trail. Please do not attempt to enter this cabin. It is for paying overnight guests only.

The Red Horse Suite sits back from the rim and some guests believe it should have a view of the canyon for the steep price, but the history and decor of this cabin is well worth it. There are also the regular cabins and the famous rim cabins that you can rent for the night. With the Bright Angel Lodge and Buckey O' Neill's cabin being the oldest occupied area on the canyon's South Rim, just how haunted can it be? Very.

Buckey O'Neill Suite and Lodge

James, Carol, and their two teenage children had reserved the Bucky O'Neill Suite six months in advance. After arriving later than planned, they excitedly came to the front desk and checked in. They were thrilled that they didn't have to wait in a line. After receiving their room keys, they immediately went to their cabin to drop off their luggage then ran out to the rim because they did not want to miss the phenomenal and ever-popular Grand Canyon sunset. After the sun went down, the whole family went to the El Tovar Hotel for dinner. Exhausted from a long day of driving, exploring some of the Grand Canyon Village, and walking on the Rim Trail, the family was ready to retire for the evening. The next morning they had plans on getting up early to hike down the Bright Angel Trail.

When they approached the Bucky O'Neill Suite's room door, Carol inserted her key card into the electronic lock. She received a green light indicating the door was unlocked then she turned the door handle and got the door opened about eight inches when suddenly the door was violently pushed shut in Carol's face from inside of the room. Carol was mortified. Was someone inside their suite? Was there a robber inside their room? James, not to be trifled with, grabbed his wife's key card and inserted it once again into the electronic lock. Again the light turned to green. James was ready to confront whomever was inside their room. He turned the handle on the door and was also only able to open the door about eight inches before he felt a hard push on the door from something inside the room before it was also slammed in his face. Now panicked that someone definitely was inside their room, Carol went running to the front desk. Upset, she told the front desk staff what had just happened. The front desk staff smiled and nodded their heads at the story. They knew that Buckey was up to his old tricks. A few individual employees working at the Bright Angel Lodge have known that the Buckey O'Neill Suite is reputed to be haunted by the great man himself.

A front desk clerk called for a bellman to escort Carol to her cabin and assist the family on opening up the rooms door. When the bellman and Carol reached the Buckey O'Neill Suite, the attendant used a special key card that he carries with him to enter into any cabin and is only allowed to be used in emergencies. The door opened with no problem and the bellman entered the suite. There was no sign that anyone had been in the room and all the doors and windows were checked to see if there was a possible break in. The cabin was secure and nothing was out of place. The bellman assured the family that everything was fine. He also told them that if they needed anything at all not to hesitate to call the front desk. All the family wanted to do now was get some sleep. They had to be up before the sun to beat the heat for their hike down the Bright Angel Trail.

Bright and early the next morning, Carol came to the front desk very irritated. This disgruntled overnight guest claimed that the phone in their room rang all night long and when they would answer it no one was ever on the other end, just static. They eventually took the phone off the hook so they could get some sleep. The front desk staff contacted the switchboard to ask if they knew who kept calling the Buckey O'Neill Suite during that evening. The employee working at the switchboard desk said that no calls had come in during the previous evening for that specific room. Unfortunately, the only thing the front desk staff could do was apologize, and the family was refunded some money for that night's stay.

The Buckey O'Neill Suite can be terrifying for some overnight guests that Buckey seems to have taken a stern dislike to. This extremely possessive ghost has also been known to harass a select few of the housekeeping staff when it comes to the cleanliness of his rustic cabin. It seems that if you do not treat his old haunt respectfully enough, he will try to keep you out. Buckey's favorite trick appears to be slamming doors directly in front of the overnight guests.

He also has been known to mess around with the bed sheets in the suite after housekeepers have already made them. His antics have scared some maids to the point that they refuse to continue cleaning this cabin. Then there are certain housekeepers who aren't intimidated by Buckey's shenanigans, but he still likes to harass them regardless. While they are cleaning his room, the door to the suite is often propped open and points out into the main hallway. Housekeepers and room inspectors will hear this door slam shut for no apparent reason. They'll just walk over to the door, prop it open again and tell Buckey to knock it off.

Sometimes guests have heard the sounds of someone walking around the room wearing heavy boots when everyone is asleep. Guests have also stated that when they are in bed, they can distinctly feel someone sit down on the edge of the bed, and when they look they can clearly see a depression on the mattress as if someone is sitting there. Buckey's ghost can sometimes be seen standing in the living room while gazing into the fireplace or just lounging on the chair in the bedroom. How do the guests know it's Buckey O'Neill? There is a framed picture of this handsome pioneer on the fireplace's mantel, and they have all reported the entity they have seen as the same man from the photograph. Just remember, Buckey built this cabin and he loved the Grand Canyon so much that even his death couldn't keep him away. You are only a guest and visitor in Buckey O'Neill's home sweet home.

As for Buckey's Lodge itself, room 6112 and 6114, including the linen closet between these two rooms seems to give the most haunt for your buck. Kay had been a housekeeper and a room inspector for around five years with the Bright Angel Lodge. She's a woman who's always passionate about her job and everything she does. She always has a smile on her face and will give a helping hand wherever it is needed. One thing that does annoy her though is if any of the linen closets are left a mess—then we see a part of Kay that will put the fear of God into anyone. Everything has its proper place and she just asks that things are put back where they belong. Kay had heard about all the stories that circulated around the park about its many ghosts and hauntings, plus she had encountered a few herself, including the alleged spirit of Mr. Buckey O'Neill when she was cleaning his cabin and a housekeeper refused to enter the haunted abode.

Inside the closet between rooms 6112 and 6114, someone or something likes to completely rearrange everything within it, and on occasions, it looked as if World War 3 has taken place with all the linens being thrown everywhere. One morning, Kay was once again trying to organize this linen closet after she found it a mess. All the housekeepers were busy cleaning the rooms after all the overnight guests had departed. No one was walking around inside the hallways and the only thing that could be heard was vacuum cleaners being used inside the rooms. As Kay was rearranging the closet, she heard what she believed was a man with a deep voice call out her name. She turned around towards the hallway to see who it was but there was no one around. Kay left the closet and went to the closest guest room in which a housekeeper had been busy cleaning and asked her if she had called out to her, but the hurried employee shook her head and said, "No." Then Kay asked her if she had seen anybody out in the hallway walking by and the housekeeper claimed she hadn't seen anyone. Kay didn't have time for whoever this jokester was and went back to cleaning up the closet.

A few minutes later, again Kay unmistakably heard someone calling out her name once more. Annoyed about being interrupted again, she went back to the same room where the housekeeper was just finishing up and asked her what she needed. The girl was bewildered and said she had never called out for her or anyone. These two women were the only employees assigned within that area of the lodge. Kay was irritated, went into the hallway, and told whatever was calling out her name to knock it off.

Many people have admitted to hearing their names being called out from a disembodied voice inside this area of the Buckey Lodge. Directly down the hallway from this closet is the entrance to the Buckey O'Neill Suite. Coincidence? You decide. This linen closet seems to take on a life of its own. Housekeepers and inspectors go into this closet to retrieve items that are needed for cleaning and making up the guest rooms throughout the day. After the housekeepers go home, the job of the porter is to pick up where the housekeeping staff left off. They have a vital role in maintaining cleanliness throughout the lodges and assisting with overnight guests needs. One of the most important jobs they are given is to walk the perimeter of all the lodges and cabins in the evenings and make sure all doors and locks are firmly secure.

In March 2014, one of the night porters followed his regular routine and walked the Bright Angel complex making sure everything was in its proper place and all doors that guests don't have access too were unquestionably sealed. As he was headed back to the front desk, taking a short cut through the Buckey Lodge, he was nearing the end of the hallway where rooms 6112 and 6114 and their linen closet are located. When the porter rounded the corner, he noticed a linen cart from the closet had been pushed out into the hallway, loaded with towels, sheets, and pillowcases that had been unfolded and thrown in a heap—plus the linen closet door was standing wide open. A half hour earlier, this now-confused porter had already inspected and secured this door. As the porter surveyed the closet, he was unnerved to see that besides the linen cart being a mess, someone or something had strewn everything else around in the room. He spent around thirty minutes trying to fix the chaos. Other porters have claimed they too have entered into this same closet to retrieve items to take to guest rooms and its neatly arranged only to return a little while later to find it completely thrashed when they have the only set of keys.

On one late morning in June of 2013, housekeeping inspector Kay was once again inspecting overnight guest rooms inside the Buckey's Lodge. Kay was going over room 6116, when a housekeeper poked her head into this room and informed Kay she had just finished cleaning guest room 6112. Inspectors started taking a special interest with this room because after it would be inspected and given an all clear, the overnight guests upon entering this room for the first time would complain that the room would be untidy. As soon as she finished her inspection of room 6116, Kay proceeded to room 6112. She inserted her key into the electronic lock to unlock the door and was able to push it open about two inches before she realized something was keeping the door from opening inside the room. Kay went and retrieved the housekeeper who had just cleaned the room and the girl couldn't explain as to what could be blocking the door. Both women pushed with all of their strength to move whatever it was that had been barricading the door. After they pushed the obstruction out of the way so they could enter the room they were baffled by their discovery. Somehow, after the housekeeper left the room, one of the rooms heavy night stands was purposely placed in front of the door to block access into the room.

Upon inspection, all of the windows in this room were locked from the inside and there was no living presence within the room, well, no one that anyone could visually see anyways. The main question is who or what was physically able to pick up and move an extremely heavy wooden nightstand in front of the door, barring entry, and then miraculously disappear from within the room with no way out.

On another evening, an overnight guest staying in room 6112 came to the front desk and claimed his room was freezing even though it was during a warm summers day and that he even had to turn on the rooms heater to take the chill off. The guest asked if it was possible if he could receive an extra blanket. A porter was sent to this room with an extra blanket in tow. An hour later, the front desk received a call from this same man requested yet another blanket. The front desk shift supervisor informed the gentleman that he would be receiving another blanket shortly and then asked him if he would like to be moved to a different room. He declined, saying he loved the room, it was just abnormally cold in there for some reason. (Most of the Bright Angel Lodge and Cabins are not equipped with air conditioners.) Later that same night, this male guest decided he wanted to stay an extra night at the park, so he called the front desk and asked if he could remain in this same room for extra day. During the summer season, the parks hotel rooms are normally booked months in advance. You're lucky if you can even find a hotel room in a town as large as Flagstaff, eighty miles away. Luckily, on this night the Bright Angel still had a few "Hiker Special" rooms. That's the name given to a number of rooms in the Buckey and Powell Lodges. The majority of the hikers don't care if there are any bathrooms or TVs in these rooms; all they are interested in doing is sleeping. So, the man staying in room 6112 was able to get the same room for a second night.

The next evening, once again the same guest from room 6112 came to the front desk. This time he informed the front desk staff that he believed his room was haunted. When asked why he believed his room was haunted, he claimed he had been having strange experiences in there. He explained that there was no reason for his room to be so bitterly cold when it is 85 degrees outside, having the room's heater on plus the extra blankets that were sent to his room were doing very little to help keep him warm. Then he said that he could clearly hear a disembodied male voice talking in his room but was unable to make out what was being said. The front desk staff told him that he is probably just hearing someone talking from within another room and that the walls in these cabins are paper thin. The guest then said that he has heard people talking from other rooms and also from within the hallway. He claimed the voice he was hearing sounded nothing like the other guests talking within their rooms.

He continued by saying that while he was lying in bed reading, he began hearing a man's voice talking as if he was right next to him. He also said that he felt as if someone was walking around his bed trying to communicate with him, but he couldn't understand anything that was being said. As soon as the voice stopped, he could clearly hear someone or something walk across the ceiling of his room. Upon listening to the man's story, the lead at the front desk told him that it was possible that it might just be an animal that got into the rafters and was just hanging out. The guest looked at her and said, "So you're telling me that animals here wear boots? I am distinctly hearing footsteps with hard-soled boots." He continued by claiming that a half hour later, there was pounding coming from the wall behind his bed, from within the linen closet between rooms 6112 and 6114. When asked if there was anything they could do to make him more comfortable, he said that he didn't mean to sound like he was complaining. He wanted to tell someone about what he was experiencing within this room, claiming he never believed in the paranormal before and his family and friends knew him as a as a hard-nosed skeptic. He would laugh and make fun of anyone who even believed in ghosts, UFOs, or Bigfoot. Now, thanks to Bucky Lodge's room 6112, he is now a firm believer in the supernatural. Room 6114 has had a lot of the same paranormal occurrences as 6112. These two rooms get a lot of calls for extra blankets because guests claim these rooms can become icy cold even on warm summer nights. These rooms have also experienced someone knockings on the room's door and when guests answer, no one is ever there.

The Powell Lodge

The Powell Lodge's overnight guest rooms are similar to the rooms inside Buckey's Lodge. Many of the guest rooms have no bathrooms or televisions and also has the shared washrooms and showers. One overnight guest room, 6126, does come with a toilet and a sink. If you want a shower you have to use one of the shared ones accessed through the hallway. However, what do you do when you rent a room that comes with a toilet, but you're not allowed to use it because it's already occupied...by a ghost? That's the dilemma you might face if you rent guest room 6126. The door to this bathroom is equipped with an old-time lock. The locking mechanism for this door is a turn-style knob and can only be locked from within the bathroom. It does not lock on its own. There needs to be a physical force to turn this type of lock and once it is locked you cannot unlock it with a key. There are also no windows within this bathroom.

One day a housekeeper was getting ready to clean this room. She went to open the bathroom door and discovered it was locked. She thought maybe a guest was still occupying the room. She glanced around the room and noticed there was no personal belongings anywhere. She knocked on the bathroom door and asked if anyone was inside. After receiving no answer, she immediately notified one of her supervisors of the situation. The supervisor called the front desk staff to verify if the room was a stayover or if the guest had checked out. She was told that the guest had departed earlier in that morning. The supervisor met with the housekeeper that was assigned to clean room 6126. The door to the bathroom was still locked from the inside. The supervisor knocked on the bathroom door, asking again if anyone was in the bathroom. There was no response. She tried everything she could think of to get the bathroom door to open. Not having any luck, she finally decided that she needed to call the park's engineering department.

When the engineer employee arrived, the decision was made to take the door off its hinges. When they were finally able to remove the door, to their surprise there was no one on the other side of the door. Upon inspecting the lock, the engineer said it was impossible for that kind of lock to turn on its own accord. The front desk staff for the Bright Angel Lodge has received quite a few calls from overnight guests complaining that the door going into the bathroom is locked even though the guest had just previously been in there. If you plan to ever stay the night at the Bright Angel Lodge and you have a medical condition that makes you have to run to the bathroom a lot, I would suggest a different room to stay in. The ghost of room 6126 does not like to share this bathroom.

The Long Walk

All of the lodges within the Grand Canyon Village have porters working around the clock. The job of the porter is to clean the interior and exterior of the lodge's lobbies. They also become the housekeepers when the housekeeping staff leaves at the end of the day. It's a thankless job. As for the night porters, their main job is to try to stay awake. If you have ever been unlucky enough to be scheduled to work any night shift, you will learn it can be boringly uneventful. The fight to keep your eyes open is technically what you are getting paid to do. There are housekeeping/porter cleaning closets scattered throughout the property of the Bright Angel Lodge. The Rim Cabins are located only a few yards from the Grand Canyon's abyss. A few of these rooms are also equipped with gas fireplaces. They are beautifully crafted cabins with great views of the Grand Canyon and the Lookout Studio. On the backside of the Rim Cabins is a long wooden boardwalk.

While working the seemingly endless nights, the lodge's porters will make a beeline straight to the cleaning closet located on the backside of the Rim Cabins. Inside this closet is the night porter's best friend and hero, the almighty coffee pot. It was in April of 2015 when one of the Bright Angels porters became a believer in the afterlife. Feeling pleased with himself that he had just finished all of his duties early, night porter David decided he would go to the cleaning closet, make some strong coffee, and continue reading from a book that he had a hard time putting down. If the night auditor at the front desk needed him for anything, she could contact him through his assigned two-way radio.

It was around 3 a.m. and it had become quite a chilly night. After David had finished making the coffee, he poured himself a cup, retrieved his book then walked over to a chair and situated himself comfortably and began to read. He would occasionally sip the hot coffee that in all actuality looked more like a cup of mud. About a half hour later, David felt himself starting to doze off. He groggily stood up from the chair and decided to prop the cleaning room's door open, which lead out towards the boardwalk, in hopes that the cold air would help him stay awake. David turned around and strolled back over to the coffee pot. He poured himself another cup of java then went back to reading his novel. As he swallowed the coffee, he heard the sound of boots walking up the boardwalk towards the room he was in. Thinking a hotel guest was out for a midnight stroll, he casually walked to the door entry to greet the night-owl. Stepping outside the door, he was surprised to find no one there. Looking up and down the boardwalk, David knew he distinctly heard footsteps on the wooden planks of the Rim Cabins walkway.

Standing at the door for about a minute, wondering where the person had disappeared to, the porter recalled that he never heard any of the Rim Cabins' guest room doors open or close. As he returned back to the chair to pick up where he had just left off with his book, he started to hear a man's voice mumbling. He figured one of the guests must have turned on the television in their room and they set the volume up a little too high. As he sat reading, the man's voice became louder and it actually sounded as if it was in the same room with him. The disembodied voice seemed like it was coming from every corner of the room. He couldn't make out what was being said, but it was obvious that someone or something was in the same room with him and it sounded angry.

It was scaring the hell out of him. David also recounted that the room had become excessively warm and now he heard the footsteps once again but this time they were in the same room as him too, and it sounded as if they was encircling him.

David quickly jumped out of the chair and his legs felt like they had become like gelatin-jigglers. He couldn't stop the trembling that had seized his body—brought on by sheer fright. The frightened porter felt like he had become a hostage within his own body, because he was too terrified to move. After what seemed like an eternity, the disembodied mumbling and footsteps finally came to a halt. Almost immediately, the sound of the boots were walking on the boardwalk again but this time they sounded as if they were headed away from the cleaning closet. David finally got up enough nerve to walk over to the door and peek out. He hesitantly looked up and down the boardwalk. There was not a living soul anywhere in sight, well not anyone that he could see anyways. He didn't need any more coffee to stay awake that night. He fled the closet as fast as he could and went back to the Bright Angel Lodge where he believed there would be safety in numbers. This was the last night this porter would ever step foot into this cabin's cleaning closet again.

The outlying cabins have had some eerie experiences as well. Overnight guests staying in cabin 6175 have claimed that the room receives phone calls during all hours of the night and when they answer the phone all they hear is static on the other end. Also in this room, guests have claimed that during the night while they are sleeping they are awakened by sounds of someone walking around inside the room. Unexplained cold spots are a common occurrence, and lights turning themselves off and on have also been reported. Guests have claimed that this room just seems to emit a creepy vibe.

The Bright Angel Lodge itself is a hotbed of strange occurrences. I'm not including the bats that fly down through the fireplace chimney to torment and dive bomb people walking around in the lobby or raccoons that just walk in through the doors and feel that the trash cans within the lodge provide them with their own fast food takeout. There is also the occasional deer that will run into the lobby trying to get away from the touchy-feely tourists. That's not the kind of "strange" I am talking about. I'm talking about things that go bump in the night and, believe it or not, during the daytime hours as well. An unexplained voice calling your name, dark shadows flying around, and being touched by something that's not there—this is one heck of a fun place.

Bright Angel's Bar and Lounge

The coffee shop in the Bright Angel Lodge opens in the summer months at around 5:30 in the morning. This is the only place within the park that is open this early where you can get coffee, tea, juice, fruits, and pastries. This is a paradise for those descending into the depth of the canyon at such an unholy hour. Then at 11 a.m., the coffee shop ends and it becomes the Bright Angel's bar/lounge. This time it becomes the hiker's oasis for those ascending from the canyon's depths. They want that beer or cocktail to wash down the dusty trails. (Whatever happened to just plain old water?) Though the coffee shop/lounge may be a haven for some, it has become a living nightmare for others. Tracy had worked at multiple places within the park. She was a housekeeper, a front desk agent, a gift store clerk, and a barista at the Bright Angel Coffee Shop. Having worked in the park for some time, she was no stranger to the hauntings that happen around the village. Tracy has been scared to death by events she has personally witnessed throughout her stay at the canyon, but this experience had topped them all.

Tracy is one of the sweetest people you could ever meet. I consider myself lucky to have met her. A very hard worker, she would wake up at 3 a.m. and be at the Bright Angel Coffee Shop by 4 a.m. to begin preparation and set out all the snacks for the early morning hikers. Tracy would always work alone, setting up the coffee shop until the second barista arrived around 5:30 a.m. One morning in September of 2013, when Tracy arrived at the coffee shop, she unlocked the coffee shops door to let herself in and then relocked them until it was time to open. She walked up the stone stairway and walked behind the bar to begin preparing that day's menu.

Since it was summertime, it was very warm and muggy inside the coffee shop—even at that time in the morning. Tracy needed some cool air, and luckily next to the coffee shop is the Bright Angel Restaurant, with air conditioning. There is an open window between the restaurant and coffee shop that is separated by two sets of wooden blinds. Not being able to unlock the front doors to allow some fresh air to come in, Tracy decided she was going to pull open the wooden blinds to try to get some cool air from the restaurant to circulate and cool off the coffee shop.

The lounge eventually started to cool down and Tracy continued with her duties. She bent down to get some milk out from the refrigerator when all of a sudden she heard someone walking up the stone staircase and coming into the coffee shop from the Bright Angel lobby. Startled, because she knew the main doors were locked, Tracy called out, "Who's there?" Receiving no response, she slowly walked over towards the staircase. No one had come in and the doors were still bolted. Tracy turned around to go back and finish setting up, when suddenly both sets of wooden blinds between the restaurant and coffee shop that she had just opened slammed shut. That was enough for Tracy and she ran out of the coffee shop and headed straight to the Bright Angel Restaurant where hopefully she would find someone living with a pulse. After regaining some composure, she hesitantly returned to the coffee shop. Later that day when Tracy went back to her dorm room, she told her roommate about what had happened. To her surprise, her roommate whom also had at one time worked at the Bright Angel Coffee Shop had the same thing happen to her. Several bartenders and waitresses have claimed to have experienced cold spots, disembodied voices and footsteps, and unexplained rappings on walls and windows within this coffee shop/lounge.

Repel the Undead

Various cultures around the world, each with different religious beliefs, generally believe in some form of an afterlife and worship a god of their choosing. Some people celebrate their deceased family members by having extravagant feasts at their graves or even exhuming the corpse to change the deteriorated clothing for newer ones. However, a large majority of the population fear the dead. Over the years, horror movies have made lots of people scared of anything that goes bump in the night even though that spine-tingling bang might simply be a water heater turning on or the wind blowing through the rafters of your house. When you hear these sounds, your heart tends to beat a little faster, you take in a deep breath to try to calm yourself and, if all else fails, you go wake someone else up in the house to go look for the boogeyman for you, all the while you're hiding under the covers so if the monster does sneak into your room while you are alone, it won't see you. Once you are given the all clear, you know that the house is safe for another night from all the zombies, ghouls, or witches looking to make you their next victim. With that being said, there are still many individuals in this crazy world of ours that truly believe that every loud noise they hear at night is something evil that is there just to terrorize them and their families.

For centuries the Navajo Indian Tribe has believed in many different types of evil spirits, including the dreaded skinwalkers, and they have some pretty compelling evidence involving the supernatural. Keeping their families and tribe safe from malevolent spirits is important to them. Ghost beads are sold in almost every gift store in the park including different areas on the Navajo reservation that borders the canyon. They are worn to protect the individual wearing them against malicious ghosts and nightmares. Ghost beads are made from berries that are picked off of juniper trees, which grow abundantly in northern and central Arizona. The berries are harvested and dried out then strung together on a string with other multicolored beads. The Navajos believe that these berries have magical qualities to ward off evil. They are sold as necklaces, bracelets, and earrings, come in various colors and sizes, and are a good conversation starter. Some people actually wear them hoping that they do as advertised, "KEEPS THE GHOSTS AWAY."

Having heard about the ghosts and hauntings around the canyon, one front desk employee at the Bright Angel Lodge bought a few hoping they did do as advertised. This employee figured more is better and would wear several ghost bead necklaces at any given time. Well, I guess someone forgot to inform the ghosts around the canyon that if the living are wearing juniper berries, they are supposed to flee in terror. While this employee was standing at the front desk, all three ghost bead necklaces she was wearing, fell off her neck simultaneously. These necklaces have a secure locking mechanism that keeps your necklace secure until you are ready to take them off. The poor girl picked her necklaces up and just stuffed them into her pants pocket. Another person at the front desk laughed at her and told her that the Grand Canyon ghosts are too smart for anyone to try to fool them with magical beads.

Messing with the Hired Help

The Bright Angel has the busiest lobby within the park. It is at this lodge where the Grand Canyon tour buses drop off their passengers. Tourists traveling to the North Rim by shuttle gather here and it has the main transportation desk for mule rides and Phantom Ranch reservations, including bus and helicopter tours. The bellman's podium is right across the lobby from the lodge's front desk and transportation desk. The bellmen have a very demanding job. They are constantly on the run retrieving guests' luggage that arrive and depart from the Grand Canyon Depot, storing bags for guests that are hiking into the canyon, moving guest's bags from one room to another, and answering endless array of questions from tourists. When the front desk staff need the bellman, they can notify them by a two-way radio if they are off the property, but if they are inside the lodge there is a buzzer they push to let him know when he is needed. These buzzers are in out of the way places and under shelves at the front desks.

One early morning, Bill, a guest service agent working at the front desk, took a ten-minute break out by the rim. That left Sarah at the front desk alone to check guests in and out of their rooms and to answer questions from day tourists. Once Bill was outside on his break, Sarah had a guest approach the counter to check into the lodge. The morning bellman on duty was Marty, who was in the back office completing his daily paperwork before the Grand Canyon Railway train arrived with its normal capacity of over eight hundred passengers. As Sarah was checking this guest in, she heard the bellman's buzzer go off. Not thinking twice about it, she assumed Bill had come back from his break and needed the bellman for something. Marty came out from the back office and walked up to Sarah and asked her what she needed.

She looked at Marty and said that Bill must have rang for him because she had been busy with a guest. The bellman looked around and said that there was no one up front but her. Sarah admitted that she heard the buzzer go off but swore she never went anywhere near it. The overnight guest she was checking in backed her up and told Marty that he had also heard the buzzer go off but that Sarah didn't push it. All she had been doing was assisting him with his room. It was also pointed out to the irritated bellman that the location where Sarah was standing, there was no buzzer within her reach.

A few seconds later, Bill casually strolled in through the lodge's back door from his break. Sarah and Marty explained to Bill what had just happened and he just laughed it off, saying that it must be one of the resident ghosts screwing with them. Marty left the front desk and went back into the office to finish his paper work. Sarah and Bill were both joking around with the guest about the ghost stories associated with the lodge when the bellman's buzzer went off yet again. Sarah, Bill, and the guest just looked at each other as Marty emerged from the office again, stood in the doorway and shot everyone the evil eye, which caused everyone to bust out laughing. The bellman's buzzer went off a few more times that day by itself but that didn't stop any of these busy and hard-working bellmen from seeing if anyone needed anything. They were all good sports about it, especially Marty, even if he was somewhat annoyed.

There are also claims by Bright Angel Lodge's front desk employees about hearing a disembodied woman's voice in the back office calling out their names, and when they go into the back to see who it was, no one is there. People also have reported hearing someone whistling an old-timey tune in the back area, but upon investigating, there is no living soul anywhere to be found.

A few steps down the hall to the right of the Bright Angel's front desk is a small museum that displays uniforms, fine china, and other miscellaneous items from the heyday of when the Fred Harvey Company managed the park. The hallway directly in front of this museum seems to have an active spirit that hangs around and likes to shove guests and staff around. A few people have "fallen" down the stone staircase that leads to the restrooms. Several of these people have claimed that they were actually pushed. I've personally witnessed people standing at the top of these stairs instantly become airborne and tumble down the stairs.

Becoming a Believer the Hard Way

One late winter's evening in February 2014, guest service agent Christina was working at the front desk alone while the shift supervisor Emily was in the back office catching up on her paperwork. Behind the front desk is a shelf where clipboards are sometimes kept. On this particular evening, there were three clipboards stacked on top of each other that held documents that needed to be inspected. Christina was checking in an overnight guest when she heard a loud crash behind her. The clerk was startled and jumped not knowing what had just happened. As Christina turned around, she looked on the floor to see that all three clipboards had fallen off the shelf, face down. Thankfully, the documents were still attached to the clipboards. She picked the clipboards up and set them securely back on the shelf. As Christina turned back towards the guest, she noticed that the guest appeared frightened and asked him if he was all right. The man claimed he witnessed the clipboards just fly off the shelf as if someone had picked them up and just threw them on the floor. Christina excused herself for a brief moment and went into the back office to tell the supervisor what just happened. Emily snickered and said that she was not a believer in any of the Bright Angel's ghost stories. Christina turned around and left the office and went back to checking in her guest. When Emily finally emerged from the back office she turned towards the transportation desk and passed the shelf where the clipboards were laying. As Emily took another step away from the shelf, the clipboards were once again picked up by something that couldn't be seen and tossed through the air and landed at Emily's feet as if to ask "Do you believe in ghosts now?"

Emily turned around and stared at Christina in disbelief. No words were exchanged at first as Emily slowly bent down and picked up the clipboards, but as she passed Christina walking towards the back office, Emily smiled and said, "I believe you."

Boo

During another evening in April 2014, at around 9:45 p.m., front desk employee Kathy was checking in a late arrival to the lodge. She was waiting by the printer for his reservation to print out when, out of the corner of her right eye, she saw a large hand rise up from behind her right shoulder trying to grab at her face.

When she spun around to see who it was, no one was there. She instantly walked towards the transportation desks back area to see if someone was somehow pulling a practical joke on her. At this time of night, the transportation desk's is closed, and all the lights had been turned off. Kathy couldn't find anyone behind the transportation desk, but when she turned around to leave, she witnessed a tall black shadow that had a human form walk straight through a thick stone wall that leads outside. Kathy kept the information from this event to herself even though it terrified her.

Later that night when it was time for Kathy to count her bank, the key to her cash drawer wasn't in her jacket pocket where she usually kept it. The zipper to the pocket was closed so the key hadn't fallen out, plus she never took her work jacket off that day due to the lobby being extremely cold because the lodge's fireplace was decommissioned for repairs from a chimney fire. Kathy and her supervisor on duty that night searched everywhere for the missing key. Kathy eventually went home and thoroughly inspected her work pants and jacket when she felt an object inside the lining of her jacket that felt like a key. Figuring there was a hole in the pocket, she searched and searched and found absolutely no tear anywhere within the jacket. How the key found itself inside the lining will remain a mystery. This happened on the same night Kathy saw the creepy hand over her shoulder and the black shadow person that disappeared through a solid wall. She just knew that everything that was experienced that night was somehow all related.

In the Presence of All

The month of May marks the beginning of the Grand Canyon National Park's busiest season: summertime. All the kids are out of school and most of the overnight camping areas within the park are open for business and quickly fill up. The North Rim is finally open to visitors after being closed after their long, brutally cold winter. The wildlife is out and about, creating traffic jams, and the parks rangers are giving many different kinds of presentations to the visitors, which include guided walking tours. Hopi Native Americans entertain tourists outside the Hopi House gift store with their hypnotic flutes, drums, dancing, and songs. If you come to canyon trying to escape humanity and get some alone time, the lodges and any area on the rim is not the wisest choice. However, as I previously mentioned, the Grand Canyon spirits and ghosts will even make an appearance during broad daylight and they're definitely not intimidated by large crowds.

One afternoon in late May of 2014, the Bright Angel Lodge's lobby became ridiculously crowded with visitors from all over the world. At one point there must have been at least seventy-five people jam-packed in the lobby and the noise pollution from people trying to talk over everyone else in this area, plus sounds of laughter and kids screaming and crying, was all resonating throughout the lodge's lobby. Anyone with claustrophobia would have been running out of this madhouse. However, believe it or not, during broad daylight and in this crowded insane asylum, several people, including tourists, front desk personnel, and the lodge's bellman, witnessed a black floating mist appear out of thin air and hover above the bellman's desk close to the ceiling. It seemed to be observing all the activity going on inside the lobby and then it slowly glided towards an air vent above a set of doors that leads out towards the canyon's rim. It once again hovered above the crowd for about five seconds and then entered into the vent and disappeared, only to leave those who saw it left speechless.

The Bright Angel Lodge and Cabins are a walk back in time. If you are coming to the Grand Canyon and are looking for a place to stay, do yourself a favor and make this lodge your top destination choice. The front desk staff and bellman are professional, attentive, and willing to go the extra mile to make sure all their guests are treated like family. Enjoy a satisfying meal at either the Arizona Room or the Bright Angel's Restaurant, or if you are just looking for a nice place to have a cocktail, Bright Angel's Bar and Lounge is the place for you, which includes live musical entertainment most evenings through the summer season. Sing along, have a drink, and enjoy this amazing historical building. And maybe, just maybe, you will get to see one of the Bright Angel Lodge's eternal guests.

Chapter 3
EL TOVAR HOTEL

On September 17, 1901, the Atchison, Topeka and Santa Fe Railway commissioned its first train to run to the Grand Canyon's Village, thus helping adventure-seeking tourists get to the country's newest popular vacation destination much quicker and offering a more comfortable ride than the uncomfortable wagons, stagecoaches, and buckboards. By the end of 1901, visitors were beginning to come to the Grand Canyon in droves. The majority of the train passengers were wealthy and expected only the finest accommodations. With not many places to lodge within the village itself and no real comfort in what they did have to choose from, the Santa Fe Railway company decided that they needed the appropriate accommodations for their higher-class patrons. The El Tovar Hotel would become the pinnacle of luxurious lodging in a landscape that was considered inhospitable at best.

The Fred Harvey Company was the key factor in making this lodge a "Castle in the Rhine." The founder, Fred Harvey, was born June 27, 1835 in London, England. At the tender age of 15, Fred Harvey emigrated from Liverpool, England, to New York City in

1850. He began working in restaurants in New York City and New Orleans and eventually opened his own restaurant in St. Louis, Missouri. When that restaurant failed, Fred Harvey worked as a freight agent for railroads and traveled through the Great Plains of the United States. He saw how appalling dining accommodations were for railroad passengers traveling to North America's southwestern region in 1876, so Fred Harvey entered into an agreement with the Santa Fe Railway to start a business providing good food and hospitality to the weary train travelers. This is how the famous Harvey Girls got their start. Young single ladies were given employment opportunities to serve food, be hospitable, and cater to the train passengers. The Harvey Girls became the signature of the West. If any reader is interested in the life of these young women, there was a movie made in 1946 about them simply by the name *The Harvey Girls*, starring Judy Garland, plus there are several books that have been published about these girls' day-to-day lives working for the Fred Harvey Company.

El Tovar Hotel

Unfortunately for Fred Harvey, he never got a chance to see or visit the Grand Canyon. Mr. Harvey passed away on February 9, 1901, in Leavenworth Kansas. To put all rumors aside, Fred Harvey himself was not involved with any plans concerning the construction of the El Tovar Hotel, as he had already passed away. Fred Harvey's sons, however, were involved with the construction of the El Tovar and bringing in the famous Harvey Girls. I bring this up because there are many myths and legends about Fred Harvey's supposed spirit haunting the El Tovar "he so loved." He had never seen the Grand Canyon, nor did he know about the future construction of the El Tovar Hotel upon his passing.

There are alleged stories of Mr. Harvey's inebriated spirit running around the third floor of the El Tovar during the holiday season telling guests to go downstairs to the Christmas or New Year's Eve festivities. There has not been any holiday parties held at the El Tovar Hotel for many years at the time of this writing. There is also a beautiful portrait of Fred Harvey hanging on the staircase in the lobby. Someone started a rumor that claimed Mr. Harvey spirit occasionally walks out of this portrait. There are no bases to any of these reports. These are just urban legends people like to tell. Most haunted places do have fabricated stories and the El Tovar is no exception.

The architect commissioned to build this extravagant building was Charles F. Whittlesey of Chicago, Illinois. Whittlesey combined the styles of Swiss mountain chateaus and rustic hunting lodges of the American West in his design of this new upper-class lodging accommodation. Using Oregon Douglas fir and native stones from the canyon, he designed this beautiful and elegant lodge. The El Tovar was originally going to be named "The Bright Angel Tavern," but during construction it was changed to the El Tovar in honor of the

Spanish explorer Don Pedro de Tobar who was part of the famed Coronado Expedition that reported the existence of the Grand Canyon to his fellow explorers. Tobar never actually saw the canyon with his own eyes. One of his men, Garcia Lopez de Cárdenas, saw the canyon and reported it to Tobar.

On January 14, 1905, the highly anticipated El Tovar Hotel finally opened for business. The high-end lodge cost $250,000 to build and it was considered the most elegant and technologically advanced hotel west of the Mississippi River. It was a four-story masterpiece. The lodge offered their overnight guests electric lights powered by its own steam generator, hot and cold running water, and indoor plumbing. Washrooms though were not yet included inside the guest rooms. There were public baths on each of the four floors that patrons could use for a fee.

Yes, even with everything the El Tovar had to offer, guests still had to use shared bathrooms back then. It truly was a simple and unrefined era in history. Give me a private bathroom each time, every time please.

The rooms also included sleigh beds, steamed heat, and telephones. In the Grand Canyon's Village early years, grocery stores and farms for fresh food and dairy products were not within reach. But the Fred Harvey Company wanted the overnight guests lodging at the El Tovar to have the absolute finest and most luxurious amenities available in the early twentieth century, which included that they serve the very best and freshest in food. The company quickly realized that if they wanted the El Tovar Hotel to be the best hotel west of the Mississippi, they would have to grow their own fruits, vegetables, and herbs in greenhouses as well as raise their own cattle and chickens. In addition, a dairy shop, bakery, and butcher shop were also established. Railroad tank cars brought fresh water for the lodges from Williams, Arizona, daily. The obviously wealthy patrons of the El Tovar had numerous luxuries provided to them that included a barbershop, solarium, roof-top garden, billiards room, separate men's and women's sitting rooms, a photography studio, and an arts and music room. These perks were not available to any other guest who stayed in more "rustic" lodging options like the Bright Angel Hotel and tent cabins. The leisure-class guests received all this for the price of $3.50–$4.00 a night (adjusted for inflation, that would be $150 today).

Since 1905, the park service has remodeled the El Tovar Hotel multiple times and now all the overnight rooms have private bathrooms. The El Tovar also boasts a very large and elegant dining room that delights hungry diners with delicious foods, heavenly yet sinful desserts, and fine wines. Two fireplaces keep patrons warm on winter evenings as they enjoy their dining experience. Murals hanging on the walls in the dining room are honoring the four Native American tribes that inhabit the area around the Grand Canyon—Hopi, Apache, Mojave, and Navajo—and authentic sand paintings and pottery fill in all the nook and crannies. A bar/lounge can be accessed through the lobby and has an outside patio facing the canyon's rim for customers' viewing pleasure. On the third floor is the Mezzanine Lounge for the guests at the hotel where coffee and tea is served in the early mornings, which also contains a piano and board games. The lobby also contains a small, higher-end gift store with elegant, handmade Native American jewelry.

Fine china was produced exclusively for the Santa Fe Railway and El Tovar Dining Room in the early 1900s. Replicas can still be purchased today inside the gift shop. The original china set was put on display inside the Theodore Roosevelt's private dining room after a more modern style of dinnerware was introduced in later years. These, however, are now reproductions because a couple of guests helped themselves to a piece of the Grand Canyon's history. While viewing the authentic china in the Teddy Roosevelt dining room, they were able to take the china off the display stands and purchase them in the gift store. Because the El Tovar gift shop sells the exact replicas of the china , the employees working at the time were completely unaware that it was the real-deal china from the original dining room.

Fun fact about that fine china: while at work, my husband and co-author of this book, BJ, who had just been recently hired for the El Tovar dining room, accidently dropped a large stack of charger plates on the floor. At least a dozen plates were destroyed beyond recognition. The sound of the crashing china was so loud that it caught everyone's attention in the restaurant, from his fellow employees in the back to the guests having a quiet, elegant meal in the dining room. His manager, who just happened to be standing near him at the time, explained to him how much money he just cost the company. Each plate was quite expensive, having been lightly plated in real 24 karat gold. Needless to say, my husband nearly had a heart attack and narrowly avoided being one of the many entities that never left the Grand Canyon and continue to haunt the park to this day.

The El Tovar is also a favorite place to stay for politicians, celebrities, and musicians visiting the canyon. There is a suite where the presidents of the United States stay called, conveniently, the "Presidential Suite." This is a breathtaking suite, and regular tourists can at times rent this room. Presidents that have stayed here include Theodore "Teddy" Roosevelt, William Howard Taft, Herbert Hoover, Dwight D. Eisenhower, Gerald Ford, George Bush Sr., and Bill Clinton. Celebrities that have stayed at the El Tovar include Albert Einstein, Mary Pickford, Douglas Fairbanks, Elizabeth Taylor, Joan Rivers, Josh Gates, Val Kilmer (who will only stay in the Santa Fe Suite), and this one musician with a funny story. An overnight guest was in the downstairs lounge reading a newspaper near a crackling fire from one of the magnificent El Tovar fireplaces. On the mezzanine level (one floor above) was a man playing the piano and a group of people singing, laughing, and having the time of their lives. The man that was reading in the sitting lounge was so annoyed at all the noise and the banging on the piano from a "horrible piano player" that he stormed to the front desk to ask them to have the noise silenced. Sending a bellman up the stairs to ask the party to keep it down, the bellman became excited to see none other than singer and songwriter Sir Paul McCartney singing and playing the piano to his entourage. Needless to say, the bellman couldn't bring himself to tell the party to keep it down. Hey, when a founding member of The Beatles decides to throw an impromptu concert, the show must go on.

When I worked at the canyon, I was always asked by *National Lampoon's Vacation* movie fans about where exactly certain parts of the movie were filmed. The scene where Clark Griswold (Chevy Chase) goes to the front desk to try to get some cash for a postdated check while inside the "El Tovar Hotel" during the Griswold's family trip to Wally World was NOT actually filmed at the El Tovar Hotel. That scene was filmed in another hotel in the state of Colorado. It's sad because the El Tovar is an excellent hotel, but alas, it's true. Don't be too depressed, though, because we're here for all the ghosts and hauntings.

Bar Fight

The El Tovar Hotel, like some other notorious hotels, has had its fair share of deaths and misfortunes within its wooden walls. In the over 110-year history of the lodge, tragic stories have had a way of showing up at the worst possible times, in the form of hauntings.

The El Tovar has an eloquent and upscale cocktail lounge and serves the best prickly pear-based cocktails in the Southwest. Tourists and park employees enjoy the lounge largely because of the intimate, warm, and cozy atmosphere, and it happens to be the only lodge in the park that has an outside patio overlooking the canyon. Alcoholic beverages that have been opened are strictly prohibited outdoors with the exception of this patio. This is a great place to come and have a refreshingly cold drink after a great day of sightseeing or to simply pass time while waiting for your dinner reservation.

On June 8, 1984, Mark, a mule wrangler working for the park, went to the El Tovar lounge with his girlfriend. While in the bar, Mark and his girlfriend got into a heated discussion, and as the argument became louder, a tourist named John thought he should intervene on the woman's behalf. Unknowingly to the would-be hero, Mark was carrying a .357 magnum revolver. Mark pulled the gun out and shot and killed his girlfriend's "knight in shining armor." Ever since the time of John's tragic death, employees and guests have reported paranormal experiences inside the lounge. These experiences have been known to occur both during the daytime and at night.

One evening in 2012, after the lounge had closed, a cocktail server was cleaning tables when she saw a tall, black shadow standing in a corner of the lounge. She glanced away quickly and when she looked back it was gone. During another occasion, while a bartender was closing up, he noticed that bar stools were being pulled away from the tables where they were placed at, but he was the only living soul in the room at the time. Terrified, the bartender then ran out of the lounge as fast as he could. Tourists and employees have claimed to have witnessed shadows moving around when no one's there or have had the feeling of someone pushing on their backs. Women claim they can feel something running its fingers through their hair; patrons say that they have walked into unexplained cold spots; and others witness silverware and drinking glasses moving on their own accord. So whenever you feel that you need a drink, do yourself a favor by stopping by this lounge, getting one of their signature cocktails, and enjoying the mesmerizing view. If one of the views happens to be John's ghost, don't be afraid, just offer him a drink and a friendly smile.

Haunted Kitchen and Dining Room

Inside the large El Tovar Kitchen, paranormal experiences torment the employees who work there. Those delicious desserts that end your El Tovar's dining experience are all handmade really early in the morning when all the guests are still soundly asleep. The dedicated bakers show up around 4:00 a.m. every morning to make that day's specialty desserts—not just for the El Tovar but for all the other primary dining rooms in the village. Marge is one of those enthusiastic bakers who loves her job. One morning, Marge was in the kitchen preparing to make that day's signature cinnamon rolls. She dusted the countertop with flour in preparation to knead the dough when she walked away to check on another item she was preparing. When she returned to continue working on the cinnamon rolls, the flour she had just dusted on the counter top contained large hand prints, smeared throughout the flour. A little annoyed, Marge thought someone was having fun with her. She looked around for the prankster but could not find anyone around. On another occasion, Marge was diligently baking when she witnessed the swinging doors leading from the dining room into the kitchen swing open and heard footsteps walk in, and once again, there was absolutely no one around. Marge hasn't been the only baker in the kitchen to have experienced strange happenings. For many years, the other members of the morning kitchen staff have claimed to have had similar experiences. One super early morning, the baking staff had to be to work at 2 a.m. due to a special event happening at the park that day. Marcia, another baker, arrived in the kitchen before anyone else did, so she decided she would start her preparation work for the busy morning ahead. When Marcia walked into the kitchen, she turned the lights on and was surprised to see an older lady standing in the middle of the kitchen looking at her. Marcia said that the lady was wearing 1920s era clothing and looked as solid as you and me, but then this lady slowly faded away.

One evening after the El Tovar dining room closed, a couple of crew members were cleaning the dining area known as the Canyon Room. Inside this room there are double doors that lead into the kitchen. As the exhausted employees were finishing up with this room, they both witnessed the double doors open and a white ball of light silently float out of the kitchen area. The two startled workers watched in amazement as this illuminating ball, which seemed to have some kind of intelligence to it, drift slowly through a closed north window and out towards the canyon's chasm, until it disappeared from view.

Low-Level Spooks

The terrace level rooms at the El Tovar are small, quaint rooms, are the cheapest to rent in this lodge, and are situated on the lowest level. Quite a few of these rooms have been known to have paranormal experiences. Lights turn on and off and alarm clocks will buzz even when they are unplugged. A dark shadow has been seen in some of these rooms. A few guests have left in the middle of the night out of sheer terror after looking into mirrors in their rooms and seeing an evil demonic face looking back at them. There is also a frequent gentleman guest that always stays on the terrace level when he visits the park. He says that every time he stays a female ghost visits him in the room he occupies. He claims she is beautiful, has red hair, and when he sees her, they always have a conversation until she fades away.

High-Class Ghosts

The Mezzanine Lounge is where the piano is on the third floor. One early morning, a male guest woke up earlier than the rest of his family. Not wanting to disturb his sleeping companions, he got dressed and walked to the Mezzanine Lounge for some coffee. This gentleman was the only person walking around the floor at this time in the morning. After pouring himself some coffee, the early riser settled into a chair near the piano. As he sat sipping his coffee and enjoying the solitude, music from the piano began to play mysteriously and suddenly with no explanation. It stopped as quickly as it started. Baffled why the piano began to play seemingly on its own, the male guest got up to look at the piano to see if it was possibly a player piano. He was shocked to see that it wasn't and also discovered that the cover for the keys was closed. A little frazzled, the man decided it was time to go back to his room.

The fourth floor, which is the top level, houses the extravagant (and expensive) suites. These chambers are uniquely furnished specifically for the titles they have been given: Elizabeth Colter, Fred Harvey, El Tovar, and the Presidential. The Presidential Suite is normally not available for overnight guests to stay in. If you want to know if there is any paranormal activity associated with any of these rooms, the answer is a definite yes. The El Tovar and Fred Harvey Suites have been reported to contain paranormal activity inside them: lights turning off and on, moving cold spots, unexplained footsteps, the sound of children laughing when no children are present, and bedding being ripped off the beds while guests are sleeping. Also on the fourth floor, housekeepers have witnessed a female spirit that glides around the hallways and stands near a large pane window, looking out towards the canyon as if waiting for her love to return. Several housekeepers have refused to work on the fourth floor due to this female spirit.

It is said that when this female spirit was alive, she was a Harvey Girl who worked as a maid at the El Tovar. During the Great Depression, President Roosevelt created the Civilian Conservation Corp to help financially struggling families have an income. On May 29, 1933, the first round of workers arrived at the Grand Canyon. One of their jobs was to reinforce the retaining wall between the El Tovar Hotel and Bright Angel Lodge. Sometime after they arrived, one of the young men met and fell in love with a Harvey Girl. This girl also fell in love with him, but when she became employed, she had to signed an agreement that said she would not become romantically involved with anyone and would remain at her assigned position until her contract expired. When her suitor's job ended at the canyon, he asked her to run away with him, and she heartbreakingly told him that she was bound to her contract and couldn't leave. Distraught, the young man carved a heart into the retaining wall so the young Harvey Girl would always remember his love for her. The "Heart of the Canyon" still exists to this day and it is believed that this female spirit goes to this one particular window on the fourth floor to gaze out at the stone wall so she can see the heart of the man she loved staring back at her.

Another room that has received a number of complaints about strange activity from guests and employees is room 6415. The main allegations reported from this room seems to be with the lights. They like to turn themselves off and on. A porter claimed that he was sent to this room for a housekeeping check. When he walked into the room, he turned on the lights from the switch next to the door. As he proceeded, he distinctly heard a click and the lights went out. He turned around and walked back to the light switch where someone or something had flipped the switch to the off position. He turned it on and went back to the middle of the room when again the lights went out. Heading towards the light switch, again the porter saw that the switch had been physically manipulate back to the off position and decided this time there was no way in hell he was going to hang around inside a room that he clearly wasn't welcome inside.

Do Not Speak of the Dead

The gift store in the lobby has a little bit of something for everyone. Here you can purchase wine glasses and beer steins with the El Tovar logo, as well as the charger plates used currently in the dining room, which also features a detailed logo of the lodge. Native American sand paintings are a perfect souvenir to hang on your wall at home as one of your great memories of the rich Native American culture at the canyon. But wouldn't a true ghost story be even better, one that you actually witnessed? That's exactly what happened to one visitor in the gift store. Jenna walked into the El Tovar gift store not really knowing what kind of souvenir to purchase. After the clerk was finished helping a different customer, Jenna walked up to the register and started a conversation with the clerk. After talking about her day of sightseeing at the Grand Canyon, Jenna asked the cashier if she knew if the El Tovar was haunted. The employee started telling Jenna of different hauntings that he had heard about. They started discussing about whether ghosts and haunting really exist when a dream box, displayed across from the register, levitated and was hurled at the clerk. Jenna witnessed the beautiful relic levitate seemingly on its own accord and get launched at the clerk. She decided against buying a souvenir and ran out of the gift store.

Across from the front desk is a staircase that leads downstairs to snack machines, a water fountain, and public washrooms. The woman's restroom has been known to creep the bejeezus out of anyone who uses it. There have been reports that the lights will turn off and on and the sink faucets will all turn on at the exact same time. One woman even claimed that while she was using a stall in the restroom, all the other stall doors began to continuously slam and the lights turned off. This guest vehemently insisted she was the only one using the restroom.

The Truth Is Out There

On top of a hill towards the southern edge of the El Tovar is a long, winding staircase that connects tourists with the park's free shuttle bus stop and the historic, all-wooden Grand Canyon Depot at the bottom. As visitors hike up and down this staircase, metal handrails assist those in need to complete this tougher-than-it-looks trek. If you walk out the front doors of the lobby and onto the porch, then walk down the steps of the El Tovar towards the overnight guest luggage drop off, look over to your right; this is where you can see the beginning of the staircase. There is a legend that on certain evenings, a dark, full-bodied apparition climbs up this staircase and will either walk towards the Hopi House, go behind it, and disappear, or the apparition will walk towards the El Tovar, climb the steps up till it reaches the front doors, then fade away. No one has ever been able to confront or approach this supposed spirit. I wasn't even going to put this particular story into the book due to finding absolutely no firsthand witnesses. It seems to be one of those "I know someone, who knows someone, who claims his uncles wife's fifth cousin, twice removed, said they saw a black shadow walking around."

If there is any truth to any of this story (don't hold your breath), this apparition might be a criminal who was shot and killed in front of the El Tovar. On July 15, 1951, three men entered the El Tovar, robbed the front desk of twelve thousand dollars, and as they tried to flee, one of the robbers was shot and killed by a park ranger in front of the El Tovar. I staked this area out for over a year to get a glimpse of this dark-cloaked wanderer with no luck. I also ran into many people waiting ever so patiently with cameras to take pictures upon its arrival from the staircase, and people wearing running shoes that thought they would physically run and apprehend it. Please don't waste all of your precious vacation time trying to catch this alleged spirit. You will have a better chance of witnessing the Loch Ness Monster playing Marco Polo with Bigfoot in the Colorado River while a UFO flies across the canyon with a banner that says "nothing to see here, people of Earth."

The El Tovar Hotel is a must-see if you visit the park. There are rocking chairs and swings on the patios, so you can sit and look at the canyon or watch all the people walk by (believe me, some of these tourists can be quite entertaining). Stroll into the lobby and sit by the warm fireplaces and enjoy the ambiance. Drop by the dining room and if you don't have time for a meal, just order one of their specialty desserts. These sweet treats are well worth the extra calories. Just make sure you keep a watchful eye out for any eternal guest that may float by.

Chapter 4
MASWIK LODGE

One quarter mile (a five-minute walk) from the Grand Canyon's rim sits the Maswik Lodge. This popular lodge is located in the southwestern corner of the Grand Canyon Village and next to the Backcountry Information Center where hikers must go to receive a camping permits if they are descending into the canyon overnight. Also, the Maswik Lodge is situated in the largest ponderosa pine forest in the world, which covers 1.8 million acres. The word "Maswik" comes from the Hopi Nation and refers to their kachina god who guards the Grand Canyon.

The Maswik Lodge was built on the same property that originally housed the old and dated Motor Lodge. The Motor Lodge was built in 1927 by the Fred Harvey Company and Santa Fe Railway. By the 1940s, as more and more people traveled to the Grand Canyon by car, the Motor Lodge had to add 36 more guest cabins to accommodate the increasing number of visitors. When the 1960s came, the park administrators decided it was time to remodel the aging Motor Lodge and give it a new look and name. Most of the 120 cabins that made up the lodge were demolished and replaced with more modern two-story hotel rooms. In all, 18 buildings were constructed, and the old Motor Lodge was transformed into the new and more modern Maswik Lodge. The Maswik has 250 rooms and fills up quickly.

A few of the old cabins from the Motor Lodge days were successfully salvaged from the wrecking ball. These relics are now being used strictly for employee housing and are off-limits to overnight guests. With this lodge nestled in the ponderosa pine forest, wildlife abounds (please remember, it is illegal to approach any wildlife in any national park). Elk, deer, raccoons, squirrels, and rabbits roam freely. Believe me, these cute animals have some serious anger management issues. Staying at the Maswik Lodge, you can have a wonderful time viewing these wild and untamed animals from a safe distance.

Inside the main lodge is the overnight guest registration desk, a gift store, a small branch of the parks transportation desk, a cafeteria, and a pizza pub. The majority of the overnight passengers who arrive at the park with the popular Grand Canyon Railway tend to stay at the Maswik Lodge. Also a lot of tourists and Grand Canyon employees tend to gravitate towards the Maswik Lodge's pizza pub. It's one of the only places in the park for guests to watch sports on a big screen television, and let me tell you, the pizza is fantastic. Even though this lodge isn't right on the rim, that doesn't seem to bother a few ghosts that like to hang out around the Maswik Lodge's property.

Want to Work Overtime?

The gift store inside the Maswik Lodge has some really nice merchandise for sale, including graphic T-shirts and sweatshirts for the whole family, turquoise and copper jewelry spread throughout the store, books about the Grand Canyon region, and decorative metal art. However, what most people don't know is that this gift store has its own resident ghost that thoroughly enjoys making items sway and the jewelry stands spin around.

One night after the gift shop closed, assistant manager Josh was busy finishing up his closing duties and went back into his office to put some items away. His office also doubled as an extension of the stock room. Above the door in this room is a shelf where extra hangers and pegs are kept in large boxes, so a one-inch safety lip was added for protection to keep anything from falling off and injuring anyone. After Josh put some merchandise away, he stopped at his desk to complete his daily sale worksheets. Josh was getting ready to get up from his desk when a large box of hangers that weighted roughly twenty pounds, which had been securely placed on the shelf above the door, came flying off towards him and missed him by mere inches. Josh sprang out of his chair and tried to comprehend what had just happened. He slowly walked over towards the shelf to inspect the safety lip to see if it had somehow broke. The wooden base and lip were still intact and Josh for the life of him couldn't figure out how this heavy box could have fallen off the shelf by itself, let alone be hurled several feet to where his desk was located.

Not long after the hanger incident, another one occurred. Josh and a female employee had just closed the gift store for the night. Josh went to the back office to finish working on the day's paperwork while the lone employee stayed out front, straightening everything up. The door between the office and the gift store had been securely closed. Sitting at his desk, Josh heard the door to the manager's office open and someone walk in. He glanced up to ask the employee what she needed when he found no one there, and before the Josh could get up out of his seat, he felt as if someone rushed up on him and he could even sense a slight breeze. Every single hair on his body was now standing straight up and every inch of him was covered in goose-bumps.

Paralyzed with fear, Josh could not only hear, but also felt the floor beneath him pulsate as disembodied footsteps headed back towards the door leading into the gift shop. With his mouth gaped opened and terror oozing from every one of his pores, Josh watched in amazement as the connecting door leading into the store slowly opened then closed. Running out from the back room into the gift shop, Josh noticed that the closing employee was on the other side of the store folding clothes. Even though the frazzled manager already knew the answer, he still asked the busy worker if she had opened the door into the office for any reason, with the girl giving him the answer he was so not hoping she would say: "No." Josh confided to the employee about what he had just experienced when the girls eyes widened and claimed that five minutes before his encounter, she watched as one of the jewelry stands that's on a swivel base begin to spin around as if a child was twirling it until it finally stopped and she had to pick up all the jewelry that had fallen onto the floor. She didn't want to say anything to him about the possibility that the store was haunted out of fear of being ridiculed. Josh and the employee decided enough was enough and left as quickly as they could.

Caught on Tape

Most buildings in the main village are equipped with brand new, state-of-the-art surveillance cameras, always looking for anything out of the ordinary, including but not limited to shoplifters, assaults, and mischievous individuals (crime is fairly low in the park, generally speaking). Law enforcement personnel sit for hours, reviewing long, boring, sleep-inducing videos. Then one day, Maswik Lodge's management was informed that someone had been stealing personal property from other employees in the back office area. Park security was notified about the possible theft and were asked to review the video tapes. The alleged crime was believed to have happened in the early morning hours when the back office had been secured until normal business hours resumed. For hours, a security staff member painstakingly watched several videos and right before he was going to call it quits for the night discovered something out of the ordinary, but not necessarily criminal. The time stamp on the tape was roughly 4:45 a.m., that's when a large stack of papers which were placed on one of the desks abruptly and semi-violently shifted and became scattered all over the desk. There had been no one in the back room for a while, nor was any window open that may have caused any air current. The officer claimed that the manner in which the papers blew around was in no way natural. This incident caused a little bit of a stir within the security department, as all of the security staff got a chance to review it. They were ecstatic to have caught this, since nothing paranormal like this usually happens where the cameras are rolling. If you looked away for a second you would have missed it. Despite the efforts of security, the phantom criminal was never caught.

Living with a Dead-Beat Ghoul

Across the street from the Maswik Lodge's front doors are the only surviving relics left from the old Motor Lodge days. These little cabins have relatively small rooms, not to mention they sit within mere feet of the Grand Canyon's noisy train tracks. The park just recently stopped renting these rooms to park visitors and are now housing for only park employees.

Seasonal employee Michelle was assigned to cabin 205 as her living quarters back in April 2013. Besides Michelle, this small cabin was also home to three other female employees. To pass the time away, the girls would occasionally tell ghost stories to each other, sometimes all night long. One evening during the middle of their scarefest, the overhead light in their room turned off for no apparent reason, but the light in their bathroom was still blazing. All four terrified girls started screaming and ran out of their home and straight to a friend's cabin and told the bewildered man what had just happened. The male friend just thought the girls were being silly and went to their cabin to make sure they were safe and to check if the light bulb had just burned out. All the bulbs were still good, so the young man walked towards the light switch and noticed that someone had flipped it to the off position. The girls all swore that none of them turned it off so the friend concluded that they had just spooked themselves with their stories. A few minutes after the young man had returned back to his cabin, the girls once again were all in their bed and resumed telling stories.

A little while later, one of the girls got out of bed and went into the bathroom and shut the door. Michelle and the other two girls continued with their stories when they heard a blood-curdling scream coming from inside the bathroom. When the girls reached the bathroom door they found it locked. The girl's screams were deafening and they feared she was in danger. Michelle kept begging her to unlock the door, but all they could hear was their trapped friend sobbing. Finally, the door slowly opened to a dark room. Michelle cautiously walked into the bathroom and tried to turn on the light with no success and found the terrified friend cowering in a corner. When the girls were finally able to get her to calm down and stop crying, the girl told them that when she was in the bathroom, she started hearing like something was hissing. Fearing an animal had made its way into the bathtub, she went to look when the bathroom light blew out and when she grabbed the bathroom door to leave it wouldn't open no matter how hard she tried. At first she believed her roommates were playing a joke on her when she felt someone touch her back—that was when she started screaming. This poor hysterical girl asked her friends to look at her back because it felt as if it was on fire. When Michelle lifted up the girls shirt, she saw three deep red scratch marks running down her back.

Another incident that occurred with one of the original Motor Lodge cabins was in July 2013, when another female employee, Abby, and her roommate, Julie, had just returned to their cabin from the employee's laundry facility. It was going to be awhile before their clothes would be dry, so they decided to go back to their cabin to prepare dinner and watch a movie. As soon as their dinner was prepared, they decided to watch the horror movie *Insidious*, which they rented from the Grand Canyon Community Library. Settling in to their own beds with the blankets pulled up and dinner plates in their laps, they began to watch the movie neither had seen before. Around twenty minutes into the film, the front door to the cabin was forcefully thrown open, hitting the wall with a hard thud. Abby jumped out of her bed and ran to the door to see who was trying to scare them, which they had succeeded in doing. Besides not seeing anyone around, there was also no wind, not even a slight breeze that could have blown the door open. Julie uttered to Abby that she remembered locking the door after they came home from the laundromat. Thinking back, both girls had remembered hearing stories from current employees about some of the old cabins at the Maswik being haunted. Abby said that both of them were beyond scared and should be inducted into the *Guinness's Book of World Records* on how quickly they dressed and dashed out of the cabin. They left their plates of food on their beds and as they ran out of the building, Abby made sure it was closed and locked. The two roomies headed back to the laundry facility to retrieve their clothes and discuss if their cabin was actually one of the haunted ones that they had heard about. The girls finally worked up enough courage to return to the cabin, but when they opened up the door, one of their other roommates, Summer, had arrived home after a long day of work. This roommate was furious with both Abby and Julie, claiming as she walked up to the cabin, the front door was wide open, which is an invitation for anyone to steal all of their belongings. Abby was trying to explain to Summer what they had experienced earlier when and the television set turned on by itself. The girls fled the room and stayed with friends that night.

Terrorizing Overnight Guests

If you think hauntings only happen in old homesteads, battlefields, European castles, plantations, ancient cemeteries, or any other old ruin, you are sadly mistaken. Newly constructed homes and apartment complexes, high rise condos, and last but not least, recently constructed malls can be just as haunted as an abandoned 1600s farmhouse. This planet we call home has many mysteries and we will never truly know all of her dark secrets. I have no doubt that every piece of land somehow remembers every dark event and trauma of ancient battles that have taken place on its soil. We do know that the Native American's ancestral Anasazi Tribe survived within the inhospitable depths of the Grand Canyon at the beginning of the 13th century, but who lived here before them? Don't be too surprised to learn that some of the newer rooms at the Maswik Lodge have become a hotbed of paranormal activity.

The newer two-story guest rooms at the Maswik Lodge are quite appealing. The rooms come equipped with single-cup coffee makers, mini-refrigerators, safes, air conditioning, satellite TV, telephones, and two queen beds, plus they are nestled smack-dab in the middle of the largest ponderosa pine forest in the world and the aroma from the trees is heavenly. The main inconvenience facing guests staying at the Maswik Lodge is fighting for standing room on the overcrowded and sometimes smelly shuttle buses. However, a few overnight guests that stayed in a couple of the rooms at the Maswik had their vacations turn into a living nightmare.

Maswik Lodge guests Will and Shawn had been planning their vacation to the canyon for well over five months. They had reserved a room at Maswik Lodge for their first night and the next morning had plans to hike down the Bright Angel Trail to the Indian Garden Campground and camp there for an evening. They arrived at the park around 2:00 p.m. and headed straight to the Maswik's front desk to check in. The two young men were pleased to find the room that was assigned to them, 6738, was ready for occupation. They pulled their car around to the front of the building they were to stay in and hauled in their luggage. Upon entering the room, Shawn felt as if the room was giving off a negative vibe. He turned around and mentioned to Will that he felt they weren't welcome there. Will laughed and told Shawn there was nothing wrong with the room. Even though he was uneasy in the room, Shawn claimed a bed, removed some items from his luggage and placed them in a dresser drawer. Both men freshened up, then departed their room to go explore the Grand Canyon Village and get something to eat. After an evening of sightseeing and having dinner at the Arizona Room, Will and Shawn decided it was time to go back to their room, watch a little TV, relax, and finally go to sleep.

When Shawn chose his bed, it was the closest one to the front door. He still felt uncomfortable inside the room and said it was as if it was saturated with bad vibes but couldn't explain the feeling in any greater detail. At around 3:00 a.m., Shawn abruptly awoke out of a sound sleep profusely sweating and his heart was pounding so hard he thought it was going to jump out of his chest. Rubbing the sleep from his eyes, Shawn glanced around the dark room and thought he saw a tall black shadow of a man standing in a corner near the bathroom. He looked over towards Will's bed thinking maybe he was up walking around only to find his friend soundly asleep. Shawn looked back towards the corner to see if the black shadow was still there but it was gone. Shawn figured he had imagined it due to him being in new surrounding but one thing he did know was that he and Will needed to be up in a couple of hours to start their hike so he had to try to go back to sleep. Around twenty minutes later as Shawn started to doze off, he was awakened from not being able to breathe. When he opened his eyes, he saw the black shadow being hovering a few inches from his face and was trying to strangle him. Shawn thought he was going to die as he felt his body starting to go limp when the murderous entity slowly let go of its grip around Shawn's throat and slowly faded away in front of his eyes.

Shawn let out a yell that woke Will up out of a deep sleep. Shawn was trying to explain everything to Will that had just happened to him. Will was annoyed with Shawn's wild imagination and refused to believe his cockamamie story that their room was haunted. Shawn stormed into the bathroom to look in a mirror to see if there was any proof of his attack when he saw deep red marks encircling his neck, but Will believed his friend might have done it accidentally to himself while he slept. Shawn was now extremely upset that his longtime friend refused to believe him, so he grabbed all of his belongings and left the room to go sleep in their vehicle. Will truly believed his buddy had experienced a rare condition known as a night terror, which is different than a nightmare. Night terrors are a form of a sleeping disorder where a person will partially awaken from sleep in a state of terror.

Will felt bad about his friend going to sleep in the car but he wasn't about to leave his warm snuggly bed and the fluffy pillows that were holding him hostage, besides it didn't take very long for him to fall back to sleep. Forty-five minutes later, Will came running out of the room screaming like a banshee that a black shadow had attacked him and he too was also sporting long red marks on his neck. Neither men would go back into the room until the safety of the all-mighty sun arose, and only Will had the guts to re-enter the room, but only long enough to retrieve his belongings. Shawn and Will went to the front desk and informed the staff about what had happened to them that night and were refunded their night's stay with apologies from the Maswik's front desk staff. Two fully grown adult men, running out of a room they claimed was haunted, does indeed appear to be a nightmarish situation, but what happened to a female guest in the same complex is truly terrifying.

Elizabeth is a young woman who was overly excited about visiting the Grand Canyon for the first time with two of her friends. Running late, the group arrived well after the sun had set, so Elizabeth and her companions decided they would just get a small meal at the Maswik's cafeteria and go to their room to crash for the night. When the friends reached their room, Elizabeth chose the bed furthest away from the door in the room while her two friends wanted the one closest to it. The girls were extremely exhausted from their long day and prepared for bed. Elizabeth tucked herself tightly under the covers and decided she wanted to read a little before going to sleep and her friends opted for the television. Elizabeth had been reading for about a half hour when it felt as if someone sat down on the end of her bed. Setting her book aside, she got out of bed and walked around it, looking to see if possibly the bed frame might be broken. She got down on her hands and knees and looked at the bed frame but it seemed to be intact.

Standing back up she noticed that her two companions had already fallen asleep. Elizabeth decided it was about time to go to sleep herself so she turned off the lights and television and crawled back under the covers of her bed, closing her eyes and quickly dozing off.

Having been asleep for roughly an hour, Elizabeth was awoken by the feeling of something crawling onto her bed and laying right beside her. Knowing both of her friends had not moved a single muscle since they had fallen asleep, she slowly but hesitantly turned her head to see who or what was in the bed with her. Elizabeth didn't see a physical body, however she did notice a distinct imprint of a head on the pillow next to hers and it looked like a body lying under the sheets with her. With her heart racing, Elizabeth closed her eyes and began to pray that whatever was next to her would go away. Unfortunately, the opposite happened when she began to feel strong, powerful hands begin to caress her inner thighs. As her heart was pounding loudly, her eyes filled with tears while she silently wept. After what felt like an eternity, the stroking finally ceased and she felt something shuffle off the bed, ending her traumatizing experience. Elizabeth knew if she woke up her friends and told them what had just happened, they wouldn't believe her.

Elizabeth had never believed in ghosts herself and has more than once criticized other people that had confided in her about their own ghost stories. She tried to convince herself that she must have imagined the whole thing. That day's journey to the canyon was long, the weather had been ridiculously hot and humid, plus they made a lot of unexpected detours, so she just must be overly tired and the best scenario was to go back to sleep and everything would be better in the morning. Even though Elizabeth was trying hard to discredit herself, she could still feel where the entity had caressed her thighs. A little while later, when Elizabeth had almost fallen asleep, she began to feel something touching her thighs again. She distinctly felt a hand and fingers touching her and this continued off and on for the rest of the night. Not once did Elizabeth try to wake her companions out of fear that it might anger the entity or possibly attack her friends.

When the assaults finally cease all together right before the sun emerged, Elizabeth's friends finally woke up to their friend crying into a soaking wet pillow. Her two companions cuddled up next to her on the bed and asked her what was wrong? Elizabeth was hesitant at first but her concerned friends insisted she tell them and after she told them what she had gone through the whole night, her friends became angry and started yelling into the room that whatever this monster was needed to show itself. When the malicious entity didn't appear, the two friends tried calling it out for being a coward. Elizabeth begged her friends to stop that she didn't want it following her home. The girls packed up their belonging and left the room. While they were checking out at the front desk, one of Elizabeth's friends inquired the front desk agent if she knew if the building they were staying in was haunted. This clerk was unaware of any paranormal happenings within the canyon but her co-worker happened to overhear the conversation, cut in and told Elizabeth's friend that he had a couple of overnight guests tell him about frightening encounters they experienced in their rooms. The clerk informed the girls that if they wanted to talk to someone about their experience, go to the front desk of the Bright Angel Lodge and look for Judy (me).

Elizabeth and her friends casually strolled into the Bright Angel from the back doors that lead outside towards the view of the Grand Canyon. I remember them walking in, looked right at me and whispering to each other. I wasn't busy at the moment and all three girls walked up to the counter, looked at my name tag, and said "Hi." I smiled back at them and asked if I could help them. One of the girls told me that a clerk from the Maswik Lodge had suggested to them to come to the Bright Angel Lodge and look for someone at the front desk with my name. Elizabeth stepped forward and asked me if I knew of any hauntings that have taken place at the Maswik Lodge. I told her a few stories of the many hauntings I knew about, assuming the girls were looking for a few places to go ghost hunting, until Elizabeth confided to me about what happened to her that night. I will never forget the terrified expression that consumed her pretty face, nor the tears flooding her cheeks. I walked out to the lobby from behind the desk, took Elizabeth and her friends aside, and told them that the canyon's rims and depths are an epicenter of hauntings. My heart broke for

Elizabeth and I gave the girls a hug, telling Elizabeth to contact me if this malicious entity followed her home. I never heard from her again, so here's to hoping Elizabeth put this whole experience in the past and has a wonderful life.

Wanna Go for a Stroll?

Other supernatural occurrences associated around the Maswik Lodge don't really have anything to do with any of the buildings. The sidewalk that passes in front of this lodge, heading north, ends at Hermit Road and has had some interesting ghost stories associated with it. There have been several reports of both tourists and park employees hearing unnatural breathing accompanied with a hot, moist breath in their ears and on the back of their necks as they stroll north towards the rim.

Furthermore, people claim to have an intense feeling of being followed and have heard disembodied footsteps behind them. Besides hearing ethereal breathing and footsteps, one more strange occurrence has been told by several witnesses that involve a tall shadow figure walking side by side with them. Creepy as it may sound, these pedestrians were walking alone on this sidewalk and noticed their shadow casted onto the sidewalk or grass by the sun. What surprised them about this was there would be two shadows as if someone else was walking with them when they thought that they were all alone.

The Maswik Lodge may be a newer building in the village and it may not be located right on the rim, but it does have a large and delicious cafeteria, a super awesome pizza pub, and lots and lots of paranormal activity.

Chapter 5
YAVAPAI LODGE

One mile east of the Grand Canyon's main village lies the Yavapai Lodge. This is the largest lodging facility within the park's boundaries. This lodge is not a fan favorite of some overnight guests, because it is set back inside the pinyon and juniper woodlands, not exactly on the rim, with a perfect view of the canyon outside its windows. It does have quite a few benefits, however, as it's close to the Grand Canyon's primary visitor center, the park's only supermarket, bank, post office, the Shrine of Ages building complex, and the historic Pioneer Cemetery. The Grand Canyon's rim is only a short walk from the Yavapai Lodge by following the marked paved/dirt trails that wind through a beautiful forest with abundant wildlife as you stroll towards the rim. That's why people come to the Grand Canyon—to walk around, look at the views, explore, and hike. Several walking trails branch out from the Yavapai Lodge heading towards the visitor center, the rim, and the Grand Canyon Village. Tourists can also rent bicycles for their entire family at the visitor center. In front of the Yavapai Lodge is a free shuttle bus stop for those who'd prefer not to walk.

After World War II, tourism within our country's national parks increased drastically. The national government eventually came up with a plan to make our homeland parks safer for the average visitor, including adding more lodging to meet the high demand. That is why Mission 66 was created. Over one billion dollars was distributed between our country's national parks for infrastructures and other improvements. The Mission 66 projects started in 1956 and were scheduled to be completed by 1966. The Yavapai Lodge was born from this plan.

The Yavapai Lodge as a whole was completed in 1972, quite a few years after its intended completion date of 1966. The reason it took a few years longer to finish was because every year the demand for more suitable guest lodging increased so the Yavapai Lodge continued to grow. The main lodge offers a large cafeteria, a better than average gift store, and another branch of the transportation desk. The overnight guest sleeping quarters are spread out in different buildings throughout a large area on both sides of the main road. The Yavapai Lodge offers 358 guest rooms that are divided up as Yavapai East and Yavapai West. The main lodge is in the parking lot that houses Market Plaza.

Haunting Is the Name of the Game

Even though the Yavapai Lodge is on the outskirts of the Grand Canyon Village, that still doesn't stop a few ghosts from haunting a few particular buildings. The eerie activity seems to be attached to overnight guest buildings 2 and 5, which were reported to me by housekeeping staff. I believe these stories to be true because both of these employees had absolutely nothing to gain by telling their stories, and when they described the chilling encounters to me, they seemed honestly and genuinely terrified by what they had witnessed.

The first frightful story of any type of haunting that I heard about at the Yavapai Lodge was relayed to me by housekeeper George. He was a seasonal employee on a work visa and was grateful to have had the chance to come to the United States and work at his dream destination—Grand Canyon National Park. When George was a young child, he had seen photos taken by his grandparents years earlier when they traveled to the Grand Canyon on vacation. Looking at pictures of a giant hole in the ground with a river running through it made the young boy fall in love with the majestic sights, and he knew he had to come to the canyon to experience nature's greatest accomplishment for himself. The park hires seasonal employees from all over the world, which gave George an opportunity to visit the United States but also offered him the chance to work at the Grand Canyon, which had been his aspiration since he was a child. George was one of the sweetest individuals I have ever had the privilege of meeting. His smile was contagious, his eyes were a shimmering snowflake, and let me tell you, his shyness was adorable. Due to him being very timid, it was hard to get him to open up about his paranormal experience when he was working at the Yavapai Lodge. George seemed fearful to even speak about anything paranormal because of his faith and upbringing. I also had to have a little bit of patience in trying to decipher certain words because of his broken English, but I was finally able to get the whole story out of him.

Late one morning in the spring of 2014, George was assigned as the housekeeper for building 5. He was cleaning an upstairs room and had sprayed a foaming cleanser onto a mirror. He left the cleaning product on the glass and headed towards the bathroom, and he felt as if something was following. A chill ran down his back and he broke out in a cold sweat. George was trying hard to ignore this creepy feeling and come up with a logical explanation, because ghosts don't exist (but he is a firm believer in Bigfoot). George turned all of his attention towards finishing up with this room as quickly as he could. While scrubbing the shower, he became consumed with grief and said that he had to fight off the feeling of wanting to cry. George claimed that he felt as if someone or something temporarily took over his body because he remembered seeing memories and images belonging to a different person, place, and time.

George didn't know what was happening to him and it all started after he felt like he was being followed. He needed to get the hell out of that room. When George finished the bathroom, he regretfully remembered that he had left the cleaning product on the mirror and had to go and wipe it off. As he approached it, George was terrified by the sight of a horribly disfigured man's face looking right back at him from the mirror. The image had the facial features of a devil with its mouth contorted as if it was screaming in agony. George dropped all the cleaning supplies, ran straight out of the room and refused to ever clean any room dealing with building 5 again. That was all George would ever say about his horrifying experience. He told me that he couldn't wait for his work visa to expire so he could return home.

Kate, another Yavapai Lodge housekeeper, was assigned to clean building 2 on a beautiful sunny day in the summer of 2013. She had been given a full list of all the rooms that guests had already checked out of. The first room she was going to start cleaning was on the second floor. When Kate reached the room, she knocked on the door three times and announced herself as housekeeping (this is mandatory), just in case someone was still occupying the room. There was no response, so Kate inserted her key card into the electronic lock to open the door. When she turned the handle to open the door, a woman started yelling from inside this room. Kate closed the door quickly, believing guests were still occupying the room. She looked through her paperwork again, making sure no mistakes were made on her part when it sounded like a fight broke out inside the room with a man and woman screaming at each other. Confused because this was supposed to have been an empty room, Kate radioed her supervisor to inform him that there were still people inside the room.

The supervisor called the Yavapai Lodge's front desk to ask if the room occupants had actually checked out. A front desk employee confirmed that the room had been vacated earlier in the morning and was clear to be cleaned. The housekeeping inspector arrived at building two and went upstairs to where Kate was patiently waiting. The supervisor knocked on the door and announced that housekeeping was there to clean the room. With no response from anyone that might still be in the room, the inspector unlocked the door and entered the room that was quite void of any living being. Kate's boss wasn't exactly in a good mood about having to stop his other duties and chase would-be phantoms. Kate swore to her supervisor that she had heard a man and woman yelling at each other from inside this particular room. Thinking back, the inspector actually remembered another circumstance similar to this one a few weeks earlier involving a different housekeeper. Her supervisor told her about several odd things that he had recently heard about from different park employees about paranormal activity that had been taking place around the park.

Several times, overnight guests staying in building 2 have been awoken during the middle of the night by the sounds of children laughing and playing outside of their rooms. When the guests open the door to shoo the kids away, all they encounter is the sound of crickets. A few of these irritated guests have stated that the time it took to get out of bed to open up the door would not be enough time for anyone to hide. Children ghosts have also been heard inside some of the rooms giggling. One guest even said that while she was sleeping she was awoken by the sound of something jumping up and down on her bed. When she sat up to see what was going on, no one was there.

The Yavapai Lodge might be a little out of the way but it's still a diamond in the rough. During the winter season, the park closes down the Yavapai Lodge due to an overall decline in visitation. The lodge does open back up briefly during the holiday season however. If you decide to make a reservation at the Yavapai Lodge and are unable to get a room in buildings 2 or 5, don't be too disappointed. The very haunted Pioneer Cemetery is just a hop, skip, and a jump away.

Chapter 6
PIONEER CEMETERY

Yes, Grand Canyon National Park has its own historical cemetery. Situated next to the Shrine of Ages, the Pioneer Cemetery had been an active cemetery until 2017, when it ran out of burial spots. To have been buried within this cemetery, there were requirements that needed to be met to even be considered for an eternal resting spot here. One of the requirements was a person would had to have lived and worked in the park for over three years. Another way was to have made a significant contribution towards the benefit of Grand Canyon National Park itself. This is a beautifully maintained cemetery and holds 305 graves at the time that this book was written. In the year 1928, the John Ivens Post No. 42 of the American Legion contributed the rustic gates that still mark the cemetery entrance to this day. The Pioneer Cemetery is set in the world's largest ponderosa pine forest and has log fencing encircling the perimeter. Inside the grounds is a dirt walking path that makes a complete loop with benches that allow visitors to sit and enjoy the peaceful beauty and watch the occasional wildlife that wanders within its borders. Included in this cemetery are the headstones of many important colorful characters that helped in the making of the Grand Canyon to become our country's most popular national park.

So just who was the first person to be buried within the Pioneer Cemetery? Well, it was actually the other way around. Have you ever heard of John Hance? He was born in 1838 in Cowan's Ferry, Tennessee, and in 1852 relocated to Phelps County, Missouri. During the Civil War, Mr. Hance fought for the Confederate Army, but was soon captured by the Union forces. He was imprisoned for a time, and after the war, Hance decided to head towards Kansas. When John Hance fought with the Confederate Army, he was only enlisted as a private, however soon after the war, Private John Hance proudly gave himself a promotion to "Captain" and it stuck. Soon after arriving in Kansas, Captain Hance became a dispatch carrier out of Fort Leavenworth. In late 1868, John Hance, his brother, and twenty frontiersmen left Kansas in hopes of better prospects in Prescott, Arizona. Traveling into the American Southwest during the 1860s and 1870s was a very dangerous time. Native Americans were being forced off of their ancestral lands and whole tribes were being slaughtered by the United States Calvary. Natives were retaliating aggressively by killing all white men (women and children included) that trespassed anywhere near their territory. When Hance's party finally arrived in Arizona on December 4, 1868, there were only twelve men left from their party, all the others had been killed by warring Native Americans. Soon after arriving in Arizona, Hance and his brother found employment working on a large cattle ranch.

At some point in time within the next decade, John Hance moved to Williams, Arizona, and by the year 1883, he traveled to the Grand Canyon to see for himself what everyone else wouldn't stop talking about. Upon arrival, it was love at first sight. Hance immediately moved to the canyon and built a cabin with a water tank near a natural spring between present day Grandview Point and Moran Point. It is also widely believed that John Hance was the first permanent Caucasian (white) settler to have lived at the Grand Canyon. While surveying the area where he built his cabin, Hance discovered an old Native American foot trail that lead down the steep walls into the interior of the canyon. The trail itself was in very poor condition, with every step possibly being his last, however this well-seasoned explorer and adventurer saw huge potential in restoring the trail. He worked long and hard to make the hiking trail accessible for travelers of any age who wanted to venture deeper into the canyon, not just view it from the rim. It is believed that Captain John Hance was the Grand Canyon's very first trail guide, having led his first tourist group into its depths in 1884.

Captain Hance is fondly remembered as the canyon's (if not the world's) biggest storyteller. John's stories barely had any shred of truth to them. Did you know that John Hance created the Grand Canyon? This is how he did it. Upon coming to Northern Arizona, John was a very poor man and all he had to his name was an old nickel. One day, he pulled that nickel out from his pocket to admire it when John accidently dropped it on the ground and it fell into a crack. Digging with his fingers into the hard, dry soil, that nickel slipped even farther into the earth. This was his only nickel and wasn't about to let it get away. Panicking, Hance ran to his cabin, grabbed several shovels and every other tool he might need to retrieve that darn nickel. Every time he would get within an inch of his coin, it would slide even farther away. Eventually, the nickel hit rock bottom, which gave John great delight. He stooped down, picked up the nickel, but when he looked up, he realized he had carved a huge hole into the earth, which we now know as Grand Canyon.

One day as he was telling this story to a group of tourists, a young boy asked, "If you actually dug it, where is all the displaced dirt at?"

John Hance, in his brilliance, looked at the boy and said, "I hauled all the dirt way over there," as he pointed to the San Francisco Peaks, which tower over present day Flagstaff, Arizona, eighty miles away. He continued, "That thar dirt is how them mountains was made."

Another time, a female tourist asked Captain Hance if he was married. His answer was priceless, "Yep, once, but my wife got her leg broke one day when we was a-goin' down the trail, so I had to shoot her." John was so convincing, that all the tourists upon hearing this story actually believed him and were horrified. The joke of course was on his audience; he had never been married.

John Hance always kept his audience riveted. An old guest book from the early days of the Grand Canyon has been found that contained some visitors' experiences from the bygone days. A traveler, Chester P. Dorland, wrote about his trip to the canyon by writing, "Captain John Hance—a genius, a philosopher, and a poet, the possessor of a fund of information vastly important, if true. He laughs with the giddy, yarns to the gullible, talks sense to the sedate and is most excellent judge of scenery, human nature and pie. To see the canyon only, and not see Captain Hance, is to miss half the show" (Campbell).

The Bright Angel Lodge's own celebrity, Buckey O'Neill once wrote, "God made the canyon and John Hance the trails. Neither would be complete without the other" (Hefley). I wish it was possible to go back in time to the Grand Canyon in the late 1800s, when John Hance was telling his stories to his gullible audience, to be able to hear his wild tales. Living in the twenty-first century, we as humans have lost so much about enjoying day-to-day life. It seems everyone's wrong if they are not politically correct or comedians are racist just because they try to make us laugh at ourselves. Let's try to remember people like John Hance, who could make you feel good about yourself, if only for a little while.

John Hance passed away in Flagstaff on January 26, 1919, from the Spanish flu. His body was brought back to the canyon by friends and buried in a little, unused area a mile east of the Grand Canyon Village. On February 26, 1919, exactly one month from the passing of John Hance, the Grand Canyon became a national park. Now that Grand Canyon was part of the National Park Service, the government started programs for civic improvements throughout the park. One of the projects would be to create a cemetery somewhere within the park's boundaries.

In 1928, the place chosen for the new Pioneer Cemetery was where John Hance had been interred. Captain Hance's grave was designated as the centerpiece for the new burial grounds. If you happen to venture into the cemetery to find the captain's grave, he is in the middle of the cemetery and his head and foot stones are purposely spaced longer than his actual plot in honor of this pioneer and his tall tales.

Before the government intervened, when prospectors or adventures stumbled across any human remains inside the canyon, they buried them where they were discovered. Even to this day, only a small fraction of the Grand Canyon has ever been extensively explored, so it's completely possible that if hikers go off any existing trail, they could stumble across the long-deceased remains of Native Americans and early pioneers.

Interred within this small but quaint cemetery are canyon pioneers, park service employees, including their family members, and Grand Canyon Village residents. There is also a large monument as you first enter the cemetery to honor twenty-nine victims of a tragic crash involving two airplanes over the eastern half of the Grand Canyon. On June 30, 1956, TWA (Trans World Airlines) Constellation Flight 2 (with seventy crew members and passengers) entered the vertical airspace that was already occupied by United Airlines DC-7 Flight 718 (with fifty-eight crew members and passengers) at 21,000 feet. Both flights had departed from LAX (Los Angeles International Airport) earlier that morning. The Constellation had departed LAX at 9:01 a.m., three minutes before DC-7 was given final clearance to depart at 9:04. The Constellation was bound for Kansas City, Missouri, while DC-7 was headed to Chicago, Illinois.

Both flights had diverted off their plotted courses so their passengers could have a scenic overhead view of the Grand Canyon. Unfortunately, both aircrafts were flying into the blind spot of the other. United Airlines DC-7 collided mid-air with the TWA Constellation. The Constellation went down on the east shoulder of Temple Butte while the DC-7 disintegrated against Chuar Butte. Both aircrafts crashed in the immediate area where the Little Colorado River connects with the monstrous Colorado River in areas that were inaccessible for an immediate rescue. Special Swiss Mountain rescue teams were called in to help with the recovery. Sadly, the would-be rescuers became traumatized for life by the horrific scene playing out before their eyes. All 128 people aboard both planes, from infants to the elderly, died upon impact. The passengers aboard the DC-7 died instantly, with only a few body fragments ever being found, while on the other hand, thirty bodies from the Constellation were recovered and of those bodies, only three were able to be identified.

Wreckage from both aircrafts are still scattered over the initial wreckage areas even to this day. The crash sites remain off limits to all visitors out of respect for the passengers that lost their lives and to prevent any theft of personal property still scattered around the wreckage site.

Sixty-seven victims of the TWA Constellation Flight 2 are memorialized at the Citizens Cemetery in Flagstaff, AZ. Twenty-nine of the passengers and crew from the United DC-7's were unidentifiable, so administrators from Grand Canyon National Park had a mass funeral on July 9, 1956, for these twenty-nine lost souls. The unidentified remains were interred in four caskets and buried within the Pioneer Cemetery.

The ravine between the two buttes where the airliners crashed has been given the unofficial title of "Crash Canyon." Even though the site is strictly off limits to anyone visiting the park, there have been quite a few individuals who have trespassed on these now-sacred sites and have come back with spine-tingling tales of encountering the supernatural as a result. The designated crash area is not part of the Grand Canyon Village, but these stories are way too good not to share with you. The two separate crash sites are now considered to be one of the most haunted places inside the Grand Canyon, as well as the entire state of Arizona itself. Rangers and hikers in this general area have supposedly witnessed apparitions walking around, white lights floating in inaccessible areas, and bloodcurdling screams pleading for help just to name a few. Some witnesses have even experienced a sudden burst of wind that streams directly down the canyon walls, carrying the sound of audible, distinct, yet incoherent human voices. These individuals who have admitted to hearing these voices claimed that this phenomena scared them to their core.

Probably the best ghost story to have come out of Crash Canyon was told by a park ranger who had a terrifying encounter one night, fifty years after the tragic event. This lone female ranger had set up camp in the ravine between where the two airliners crashed. The ranger was sleeping inside her tent, when out of nowhere she heard the sounds of multiple people talking. It was startling for her because it was the middle of the night and this area was off-limits to the everyday visitors including Colorado River rafting groups. When the ranger opened the outside flap of her tent, she saw more than a dozen people walking up a trail, wearing 1950s era clothing. They were talking amongst themselves and behind them were five Native Americans, and none of them seemed to have notice the ranger or her tent. After this strange parade of people disappeared from sight, the sole ranger cautiously crawled out from her tent to see where they had gone but everyone had mysteriously vanished.

There have been reports of a woman in black clothing seen at the memorial for the United Airlines victims in the Pioneer Cemetery. She is seen knelt down in front of the monument, weeping. If anyone tries to approach her, she vanishes into thin air. There is also a feeling of sadness and despair that encompasses the area around this memorial, but would you expect anything less from such a horrible tragedy?

There are many other notable historic figures buried within the Pioneer Cemetery that helped make the Grand Canyon the vacation destination that it is today. Peter "Pete" D. Berry first arrived at the Grand Canyon in 1890, after attending his brother's funeral in Flagstaff, Arizona. Berry had heard that some miners were relocating to the canyon with high hopes of striking it rich with newly discovered copper ores. Berry and a couple of other men decided to venture towards the canyon and ended up staking copper claims on Horseshoe Mesa at 2,500 feet below Grandview Point. After mining for a few years, Pete Berry soon realized that the best way to make it rich at the canyon was to go into the increasingly demanding hospitality business. By 1892, Berry had constructed the then-popular Grand View Hotel, which was located ten miles east of today's Grand Canyon Village. When the train from the Atchison, Topeka and Santa Fe Railway started bringing visitors to the Grand Canyon Village in 1901, the majority of the tourists decided to lodge within the village area. That was financially devastating for the Grand View Hotel due to it being so far away from the main village. By 1916, the Grand View Hotel was out of business, and in 1929, the old hotel was demolished. Berry continued to live and work on odds and ends at the canyon with his beloved wife Martha by his side. Martha Berry passed away in 1931 of blood poisoning and a year later Peter Berry passed away from cancer. Both are buried in the Pioneer Cemetery.

Ralph Cameron was one of the first pioneers of the Grand Canyon and a successful businessman as well. He arrived at the South Rim in the year of 1883. Cameron was good friends with Pete Berry. In the 1890s, Cameron, along with a working crew, constructed the Bright Angel Trail and even charged visiting park guests a whopping one dollar access fee if they wanted to hike down it (that is equivalent to $28.45 today). Cameron was a real estate swindler and also "salted" mining claims with imported minerals and set up fake mining equipment. Ralph Cameron was very much against the Grand Canyon becoming a national park. His logic was that if the canyon was to become a national park, he would be out of a lot of money in his business scams that he was investing in around the area. When the Department of the Interior declared the Grand Canyon a national park in 1919, Cameron was now considered a trespasser and had to find a new home. On February 12, 1953, at the age of 89, Ralph Cameron passed away while living in Washington D.C. His family was able to bury him at the Pioneer Cemetery near his old friend Peter Berry. Could his spirit be one of the ghosts that haunt this cemetery today?

William Wallace Bass was born in Selbyville, Indiana, on October 2, 1849. When he was in his early teenage years, Bass learned carpentry and studied telegraphy. By the time he was seventeen years old, he was able to obtain a job as a conductor on the Erie Railroad. Bass was sickly in his early years of life, so as he grew older, his health progressively deteriorated. At the age of twenty-seven, Bass went to see a medical doctor who discovered that Bass was suffering from a heart aneurysm. The prognosis didn't look good, so the doctor suggested that William might live a little while longer if he relocated to the arid American Southwest region.

In July of 1883, William Bass moved to Williams, Arizona, and began to look for work on the railroad. Unsuccessful at finding employment with the railroad, he had to settle for any odd job he could find around the area. After having moved to the dry climate of the southwest, Bass's health miraculously started to improve. As time went on, Bass went into cattle ranching north of Williams. During his time as a wrangler, he became friends with the local Havasupai Tribe. In the autumn of 1883, some of the Havasupai scouts escorted William Bass to see the Grand Canyon. Upon seeing the giant chasm, Bass decided to make the canyon his new home and built a small cabin near today's Havasupai Point.

Bass also improved an old Indian path that lead into the canyon and named it Mystic Springs Trail. He also began to call himself "Captain" just like his new buddy, John Hance. Captain Bass eventually established a river camp, built a rock cabin, and constructed a wooden boat to cross the Colorado River at a serene area so he and his passengers could have new adventures exploring the North Rim. He named the spot where his boat was located "Bass Ferry." As time went on, Captain Bass opened up a stage line between Ash Fork, Arizona, and the Grand Canyon. He also opened up his own home to tourists from all over the country.

One of his home visitors was a young music teacher from New York City named Ada Lenore Diefendorf. Soon a romance blossomed between the two, and by 1894 William and Ada had married and raised four children at the canyon's rim. They were the first white couple to raise a family at the Grand Canyon. Ada was a strong, independent woman, but found living at the canyon exceptionally hard. Ada's daily life had become non-stop cooking, cleaning, taking care of all their livestock, and raising the children alone for most of the time. Laundry day for us in the present day generally means ninety minutes of inconvenience. For Ada, laundry day was a torturous three-day excursion. Just to wash her families clothing and bedding, Ada would have to travel fourteen miles round trip on a mule and travel down the steep, dusty trails into the canyon's searing heat to the shores of the Colorado River. In those days, there was no Glen Canyon Dam to hold back the flow of water, so the mighty Colorado River was normally full of red dirt and sediment and it's conceivable to believe that the clothes were actually dirtier after their washing. The Bass family was instrumental in making the Grand Canyon what it is today. There is an antique child's rocking horse on display at the small museum at the Bright Angel Lodge that belonged to the Bass children. On March 7, 1933, William Bass passed away at age 84 from a cerebral hemorrhage. He wished for his ashes to be spread over Holy Grail Temple, which lies inside the canyon. Ada passed away in Phoenix, Arizona, on May 5, 1951. This great woman is buried within the Pioneer Cemetery.

The Pioneer Cemetery is considered private property of the National Park Service, however they do allow park visitors to explore the grounds and gravestones. It is off limits to all visitors after sunset (unless the park service has a special event occurring). Do not vandalize any property whatsoever within any national park. It is a crime and the Grand Canyon has its own jail and judge.

Cemetery Fun

Many people come and walk through this historic cemetery looking at all the aged tombstones, admiring the different styles that families chose to decorate the graves of deceased loved ones, and wondering how some passed away. Many visitors snap photographs of graves and the surrounding area adjacent to this cemetery. After the visitor returns home and looks through the many pictures that were captured, they are shocked to see strange, unexplainable figures lurking in the photos that weren't there when the picture was originally taken. One such photo was taken in the northwestern section of the cemetery. A man and woman had been walking through the cemetery one evening and noticed an unexpected exit in the back of the graveyard that entered into the surrounding forest. As the couple casually walked around admiring the view, they took out their camera and began snapping pictures of the cemetery and forest. After they returned back to their hotel room, boredom set in, so they decided to look at the pictures of the canyon and village that they had taken that day. To their absolute shock, they captured a photo of either a elderly man or woman with a severely hunched back, holding a walking stick and hovering over a grave in the cemetery; and they could see trees and gravestones through the image. The couple claimed that they were the only people there. They tried to debunk the picture as an optical illusion or matrixing but were unable to do so. They decided to go back to the exact same spot the next day at the same time to take more photos to see if it they could recapture the image. After taking several more pictures, they were unable to debunk the image of the hunchbacked ghostly image floating over the grave.

You're Not Welcome Here

Kevin was at the cemetery one afternoon with his wife, Debby. They like to travel around the country and take pictures in old, abandoned, and historic cemeteries, and one of Debby's hobbies is "stone rubbing," which involves tracing gravestones with paper and chalk. Some tombstone rubbers have claimed that on older headstones of the deceased, the person that was buried on that spot's image will eventually appear on their gravestone, and you can sometimes capture their facial features with the rubbing of the chalk on the paper. While Debby was tracing some gravestones, Kevin just walked around snapping pictures of anything that caught his attention in the cemetery. They had been there for about an hour and it was approaching dusk, so Debby called out to Kevin for them to call it a night. As Kevin started walking towards Debby, he would occasionally turn around and snap a picture behind him. Kevin claimed that it started feeling eerie inside the cemetery as the sun began to set and wanted to capture that perfect picture of the darkness falling. When he reached the spot where Debby was at, Kevin turned around and snapped several more pictures from where he had been previously standing when his wife called it a day.

Looking at the screen on his camera, Kevin turned towards Debby and told her she needed to look at a couple of pictures he just snapped and tell him if she sees anything unusual in them. Debby walked over to Kevin and they both looked over the photos he just took and noticed a very large singular orb giving off its own light. Jonathan said each picture seemed as if this orb was following him. Debby suggested Kevin take another picture in the area they were standing. After the picture was taken, they both checked the screen and within two feet of them, was the same exact orb. Debby became frightened and told Kevin that she wanted to get the hell out of there. They were quickly walking towards the front gate of the cemetery, but Kevin would occasionally turn around and take a picture. As suspected, the pictures proved to them that the orb was still following them, but to the frightened couples surprise, the orb's light that it was emitting was now illuminating into different colors. Several pictures showed it went from a bluish white to a bright purple and then another photo showed it went from purple to a vibrant red and had increased in size. Upon exiting the cemetery grounds, Kevin turned around and took one last photo of the cemeteries front gate and captured the orb, hovering inside the entry to the cemetery but not beyond its perimeters. This incident didn't stop the couple from their hobby of finding historic cemeteries and stone-rubbing headstones, but they are now more aware that some cemeteries have what is called a spirit guardian. and if they feel unwelcomed, they pack up and leave.

Cry If You Must

If time permits and you are able to take a stroll through the Pioneer Cemetery, after you enter the front gate, look over to the left and you will see the graves of two young lovers who had worked in the park and died together in a tragic car accident. Their families decided to have them buried next to each other. At this grave site of these two sweethearts, severe depression has been known to affect many visitors right down to hard-nosed men who claim they don't cry and nothing can upset them. Disembodied sounds of crying have also been heard around this grave and the unknown woman in black from the United Airlines Memorial has also been seen at the joint grave site of the two lost loves.

Sadie had been employed at the park for roughly a year. In the summer of 2014, Sadie was transferred to work at the Yavapai Lodge's cafeteria and found solace in taking a short walk to the Pioneers Cemetery and sitting on a bench amongst the tombstones on occasion. One day, Sadie decided that she was just going to walk around and see who was buried at the different grave sites. She was casually walking around the western perimeter of the cemetery when she felt a wave of severe depression consume her. The feeling became so intense that Sadie began to sob uncontrollably, however she was confused because she couldn't figure out why she had become so emotional. She began to walk faster to get out of this particular area when she heard someone walking behind her. Sadie thought that she was the only person in the cemetery at that moment, so she quickly spun around to see who else had entered the cemetery. She glanced around the entire cemetery to see if she was still all by herself and she was. As Sadie continued walking, once again she could clearly hear someone's footsteps crunching on the dry grass and pine needles as if they were walking right behind her. Sadie was terrified and started running towards the front gate to get out of the cemetery but could also hear the footsteps of someone she couldn't see running as if to keep up with her.

As soon as she exited through the cemetery gates, the overwhelming sadness and disembodied footsteps completely stopped. Sadie was traumatized by this experience and told everyone that she would never again return to the Pioneer Cemetery under any circumstances. The odd part is, I have met a few people that have claimed that they, too, have experienced this exact same phenomena that Sadie had encountered, even during broad daylight when the sun is high in the sky and everything appears at peace.

Get Out

During a warm and clear summer's evening in July 2013, a few park employees who had all heard of the rumors going around about people being attacked physically and emotionally at the Pioneer Cemetery decided that they would go there to prove these claims of paranormal experiences were false. Well, it sounded like a great idea on paper, but it didn't go quite as planned. While these ghost hunters were investigating, they unknowingly became fresh targets for the playful spirits of the Pioneer Cemetery. It was quite late and there wasn't much moonlight, but just enough so they wouldn't trip on the grave stones and various water sprinkler spigots. The group first went towards the western boundary of the cemetery (where most of the hauntings are alleged to take place). With all of them standing still, they could easily hear if anything was out of the ordinary. One member of this group happened to be looking out towards the pine tree forest when she saw multiple black shadow figures quickly darting back and forth behind trees. Around the same time, another member of the group clearly heard Native American drums and chanting coming from the same area as the shadows, but deeper within the forest.

As the amateur investigators were comparing notes, one of them took out a flashlight and shined it into the woods where they were observing the shadows and listening to the phantom chanting. At first glance, they didn't see anything out of the ordinary, so it was decided it would be best to turn the flashlight off for the moment. Almost immediately, everyone in the group began to see more and more shadow people dodging behind trees, so they immediately shined the flashlight out towards that area. As soon as the flashlight was turned back on, the dark shadows seemed to just disappear. It was concluded that they would get better results if they kept the flashlight off and they were indeed proven right. This ghost hunting team was now able to witness an incredible display of multiple shadows getting closer to the cemeteries boundary where they were at and now felt threatened. Everyone in the group decided it was finally time to get out of there. When they almost reached the front gate to the cemetery, one of the female members had her hair pulled very hard from something above her. She said the pull was so strong, she believes some of her hair was actually pulled out from the roots.

This particular group of paranormal investigators soon realized that they were the ones being investigated that night and they weren't welcome inside the cemetery.

As you can see, this cemetery has its fair share of paranormal activity. The National Park Service has programs in the evenings at the Shrine of Ages and at the McKee Amphitheater on warm evenings. One of the programs is called "The Moonlit Cemetery Walk." It is a wonderful program to teach people about those buried within the cemetery. A park ranger is dressed as the Grand

Canyon's famed John Hance and guides you to different graves, and the stories he tells are a fantastic and knowledgeable history lesson for all ages. I recommend this rare program to anyone who comes to visit the Grand Canyon.

Chapter 7

TRAILER VILLAGE

Trailer Village is located in the easternmost part of the Grand Canyon Village. Located near the Yavapai Lodge and the General Store, Trailer Village is also adjacent to Mather Campground and is set back in a pine forest. This RV park is located roughly a half mile from the rim. Trailer Village is divided between tourist RV camping and park employee housing. In general, this is a quiet, serene area away from all the hustle and bustle of all the tourists at the rim. Elk and deer seem to own this area and they allow us to occupy their land. I say this because when I lived in Trailer Village, I would be chased back into my trailer room by bully elk that didn't want people among them at that moment. I was literally trapped in my own room until the elk saw another unsuspecting human to torment. Squirrels, rabbits, raccoons, coyotes, ravens, and other various canyon creatures hang out in Trailer Village. Pine, pinyon, and juniper trees are everywhere. But what most campers in Trailer Village don't realize is that this supposedly peaceful area is an open portal to the paranormal.

Trailer Village is open to the public and guest are welcome to walk down all streets and trails. Please be respectful to all those that are camping and living here.

Opened Door to Another Dimension

Trailer Village is home to quite a bit of unexplainable occurrences. For some reason, P Street and R Street seem to have the most claims of paranormal sightings. Let's begin with a very strange story that happened on R Street during the supermoon in June of 2013. P Street used to house a laundry facility for the use of park employees only. Brandon and Ellen were a husband and wife that both worked in the park. They didn't own a car, so they would walk or take the park's free shuttle bus to wherever they needed to go. On June 23, 2013, at about 9:30 in the evening, they decided to do some laundry. They preferred to go later in the evening because this little laundromat was normally packed with employees washing their clothes and at that time of night there was more of a chance for an empty washer and dryer. As they left their trailer room, Ellen noticed how bright it was outside, compliments of the supermoon. You could see everything right down to the pebble lying on the ground. Down the side streets in Trailer Village, there are no street lights. The main entrance road does, however, have a few lights to see which street you are approaching. The area around Flagstaff and the Grand Canyon is considered an International Dark Zone, which means that many towns within the upper elevations in Coconino County reduce light contamination so that stargazing can be spectacular. It's a fantastic idea and I think every state should have a mandatory designated dark zone.

This warm night in June would eventually become Ellen's very own *The Twilight Zone* episode. Brandon and Ellen were able to start their laundry right away. Luckily for them, there was only one other person in the laundromat that night. It was a sigh of relief for Ellen because she was extremely tired from her long day at work. Having gone to work at 7 a.m. that morning, all she wanted to do was go to bed and snuggle with her pillow. When it came time to switch the clothes from the washers to the dryers, she asked her husband if he wouldn't mind if she went ahead, back to their room, so she could get some sleep. Brandon told her to go ahead and that he would finish up with the laundry.

Ellen quickly left the laundry facility, which is located on P Street and cut diagonally across the R Street trailers. As soon as she reached R Street, Ellen turned right and started walking down the dark street towards her home. Ellen's trailer was almost at the end of R Street, so she had a bit of a way to go. As she started walking, she came to an abrupt halt. Ellen could only see two rows of employee trailers on both sides; after that everything on the road beyond the two set of trailers was nothing but a black void. Ellen could not see any kind of a light source coming from where her trailer was at. All of the employee trailers are equipped with outside porch lights, which meant Ellen should have been able to see at least five more rows of trailers on both sides. She turned around and looked down the other way on R Street, where she was just at, and all the lights were still on. Ellen couldn't comprehend why she couldn't see anything going down the street where she lived. Believing there was some kind of a power outage towards the end of R Street, she decided to go back to the laundry room to have her husband escort her home. He had the flashlight and he better not even consider saying he wouldn't walk her home, if he did it would mean his untimely death—and not because of a ghost or anything paranormal.

When Ellen walked back into the laundry room, she explained to Brandon that there was no lighting down R Street and she needed him to walk her home. Brandon was a little annoyed and told Ellen that she should know that if there was any kind of power interruption within Trailer Village—everyone loses power, not just a select few trailers. Ellen didn't care. She told him what she saw, or should I say didn't see, and he was walking her home cause she felt uneasy. As the two reached R Street and turned right, all the employee trailers down to the end of the road had their outside lights on, and the supermoon was high in the sky, drenching the canyon with its magnificent brightness. The moonlight was even illuminating all the pine trees and their needles. That's when Ellen realized, even if there was a power outage, she should have been able to see all the way to the end of the street because of the supermoon and the immensely bright light it was giving off. Brandon was giving Ellen a hard time and she told him that she will be able to prove that the power had gone out because when would they enter into their room, their alarm clock should be flashing the time at 12:00 like it does during any power interruption. When they entered their room, the clock wasn't flashing and read 10:15 p.m. Ellen immediately looked over towards the computer and it also had not experienced any power outage. What Ellen experienced and saw has haunted her to this day. She has always wondered: if she had decided to continue to walk into that black veil trying to reach her trailer, could she have been teleported to another dimension or transported to another era in time?

Murder on the Rim

Even in a peaceful area like Trailer Village, death has its way of making its presence known. Jane was a member of the Hopi

Nation and was residing in an employee trailer on R Street. Jane was a beautiful young girl who loved to be surrounded by her friends. It's a bragging point for most to be able to say that they have worked and lived at one of the seven natural wonders of the world, but for those who don't live here, they don't realize that for the employees who are here twenty-four hours a day, seven days a week, they need something more to do. The closest major city is Flagstaff, Arizona, which is almost ninety miles away; one way. Even the small town of Williams, Arizona, (known as "the Gateway to the Grand Canyon") is over sixty miles away.

Boredom can set in very easily especially for the younger generation, so when you hear that someone is throwing a party or having a bonfire, it can be a big sigh of relief that you won't be spending another night alone in a cramped, compacted room with nothing fun to do. Jane was always looking for things to do and unfortunately she would hang out with some unfavorable people if it meant she didn't have to be alone. One of Jane's friends was concerned about her partying lifestyle and tried to warn her about being careful with the parties and who she became friendly with.

In June 2001, Jane had been invited to a party at a friend's house. Jane's friend Mary had also heard about the party but had a strong feeling that something bad was going to happen. Mary begged Jane not to attend it, but of course, out of pure boredom, Jane choose to go. Later in the evening, when the party was winding down, Jane decided it was time to go home and invited a fellow co-worker, Mike to accompany her. That would be the last time anyone would ever see her alive again. Jane's body was discovered hidden under the bed in her trailer room, wrapped up in a bed sheet, stabbed multiple times, which ultimately resulted in her death. The police searched Mike's possessions and discovered a knife with blood on it. Mike was arrested and pled guilty to the killing of Jane. The murder shocked the small community in the Grand Canyon Village. Jane's friend Mary wonders to this day if there was more she could have done to prevent this horrible tragedy. Many paranormal researchers believe that when a person dies while suffering from extreme physical and mental trauma, their soul cannot or refuses to rest at peace, which seems to be the case with Jane's restless spirit.

Adam and Olivia were engaged to be married. Both worked for the park and were able to get a room together on R Street in Trailer Village. The employee trailer housing here is made up of numerous single-wide trailers that have each been broken down into four very small units. Each unit somehow contains a queen-sized bed, a desk, a sink, and a bathroom. Squirrels, rabbits, and occasionally a raccoon burrow under the trailers so residents can feel and hear the critters crawling around directly underneath them. The squirrels scratch at the bottom of the floors, trying to dig holes to get into the rooms.

One day, Olivia had the day off from work and was lounging around in bed, watching DVDs on their computer. As Olivia was resting in bed, she felt something under her bed pushing it up, not the whole bed, just certain areas. After it happened a few more times in a matter of five minutes, she got off the bed and looked under it to see what could be causing the bed to shift and move. Olivia wasn't able to see anything under the bed and then it crossed her mind that one of those damn squirrels had somehow made it into the room and burrowed inside the box spring of the bed. She looked all over the floor in the room for any hole that a small animal could have made but was unable to find any evidence that her room had an intruder of the four-legged variety. Olivia laid back down and continued watching the movie. Within a couple of minutes, the mattress once again felt as if it was being lifted by something underneath it, however she could also feel it slightly shake as if a small earthquake had just occurred. Jumping off the bed once again, Olivia knew she wasn't imagining it and that something out of the ordinary was going on inside the bed. Olivia reached for her flashlight and upon turning it on, conducted an extensive search in hopes of finding the exact cause of why her bed was moving. After moving the bed around, she became frustrated from not being able to find any answers.

When Adam finally came home from work a few hours later, he instantly regretted not pulling a double shift. As soon as he walked through the door, Olivia demanded Adam find the wild animal she claimed had taken up residency inside their bed. Adam did the whole eye roll thing, but to shut Olivia up he played along by flipping both the mattress and box spring over to find what could be the problem. Unfortunately, both were completely intact with no vermin in sight. Adam gave his fiancé a hard time about her wild imagination for several days until he personally experienced the bed rising and falling on its own while Olivia was at work.

A week later, Adam and Olivia were invited to dinner at their friends Nate and Heidi's house. Nate and Heidi had both been employed at the park for several years and knew a lot about the history of the Grand Canyon and the village. After dinner, the two couples sat around and talked about work and the subject of ghosts and hauntings came up. Olivia felt comfortable enough to confide in her host and hostess about their bed seemingly taking on a life of its own. Olivia had explained how they thought it might have been a squirrel or mouse but have been unable to find any proof. Heidi looked at Nate and said, "You need to tell them." Nate was hesitant at first but eventually told Adam and Olivia that the trailer they were residing in was where a gruesome murder had taken place twelve years earlier. Nate told them the story about Jane's death, plus how and where her body was discovered. Nate believed that the pushing up of the mattress is possibly Jane's restless spirit still trying to escape her fate, or maybe just her trying to scare people out of her room. Hopefully one day Jane will find eternal peace. Until then, she will probably continue to haunt the trailer where her life was stolen from her in such a cruel way.

Just Passing Through

In-between the trailers of P and R Streets, employees have witnessed bluish-white apparitions floating down the streets at night and have even seen them drift into nearby trees and then disappear without a trace. In the immediate forest that encompasses Trailer Village, disembodied voices at times are heard screaming and chanting indecipherable words. So far, nobody has been able to make out what is being spoke. One employee that lived on P Street claims that one evening as she was looking out her trailer window, she observed two very large black shadows floating down the street. The apparitions gave the illusion that they were walking, but in actuality they were gliding through the air just inches above the ground. This terrified resident claims she has witnessed these two phantoms a total of five times during her stay in Trailer Village. She is always fearful when she sees them and believes they are malevolent creatures.

Another bizarre sighting with multiple witnesses involves bright white balls of light floating all around the vicinity of Trailer Village. These orbs seem to have some kind of intelligence about them. Several people living in and around Trailer Village have watched as these orbs hover near windows as if they are peeping toms. These bright orbs have also been witnessed around the area where overnight guests park their RVs. The Grand Canyon does have fireflies, however there are many different species of these insects and the genus of the ones west of the Rocky Mountains do not glow, which eliminates them as a possibility and these balls of light can even be seen in the winter when insects are not around.

Unprovoked Attack

Another employee unit on R Street appears to have something sinister living in it. Brian and Christie had been living in their room for around two months. As soon as they moved in, strange things started to happen to them. They brought their pain-in-the-butt but beloved family cat to live with them at the canyon. Almost immediately upon moving in, their cat started acting strangely. The cats eyes would seem to follow something that Brian and Christie couldn't see. The cat would hiss and hunch its back up at something they could not see and almost daily upon returning home from work, Brian and Christie would find their trembling cat hiding in the bathtub behind the shower curtain. If they succeeded in removing him from the bathtub, wherever they sat him down, he would immediately run back to the tub.

Christie had worked earlier in the day and had been resting in bed, anxiously waiting for Brian to get home from work. It had been a very warm day, and with no air conditioning provided inside the trailers, the room might as well have been located in the depths of hell. (It's possible that purgatory was cooler than these trailers.) Brian finally walked through the front door and Christie jumped out of bed to greet him. Brian surprised Christie when he told her to get dressed and that he was going to take her to the Arizona Room for dinner. As Christie was getting ready, Brian cried out, "What the hell happened to your back?."

Christie replied, "What do you mean? There is nothing wrong with my back."

Brian exclaimed, "Well then explain to me. How did you get those huge scratches that are going down your back and why are they bleeding?"

Christie looked in the mirror and was horrified. Down her back were three large scratch marks around eight inches in length. Each individual scratch had broken the skin and they were oozing blood. Brian thought they looked like giant claw marks, but they were too large for their cat to have done this. Christie didn't feel anything and would never have known about the scratches if Brian hadn't seen them. Brian, concerned about these abrasions, put antiseptic cream on the scratches to prevent infection. About an hour later, the scratches on Christie's back began to severely burn as if it had been set on fire. It took several days before the scratches began to heal. Christie now sports three scars from where she had been attacked. After this initial incident, Brian began to notice scratches appearing on his body. The bathroom sink faucet started turning on by itself and the bathroom door would open and close on its own. Brian and Christie eventually left the park and moved to a different state. They have never been able to logically explain all the creepy experiences while in their Trailer Village room.

Trailer Village is set in a beautiful forested area. Don't let any of these haunted spots ruin your visit if you're planning a trip with an RV and want to stay at Trailer Village. If you decide to walk around this area, especially P and R Streets after dark, keep a watchful eye out. You just may become one of the lucky few who might catch a glimpse of the eternal wanderers.

Chapter 8
HOPI HOUSE

Arizona is home to a large Native American population and also contains the largest reservations in North America, the Navajo and Hopi Nations. Almost everywhere that you choose to visit in this state, you will be able to observe the many different cultures, lifestyles, and roles that Native Americans have contributed in making the American Southwest the magical travel destination that it is today. One of these stopovers is the Hopi House, within the main village of course.

Every morning for thousands of years, as the sun rose over this mostly desolate and arid land, began a new attempt of survival for the many different Native American tribes including the Hopi. Waking up meant a new endeavor at trying to find enough food and water to nourish their families, which also included seeking out adequate shelter from the desert's summertime sizzling heat. They also had to deal with heavy monsoonal rains, mudslides, and forest and brush fires, while protecting their precious crops of corn, beans, squash, cotton, and tobacco. They did all of this while dealing with the many desert poisonous snakes, Gila monsters (one of the only venomous lizards on the planet), deadly scorpions living in every nook and cranny, sickness, and widespread disease such as small pox and yellow fever and protecting their loved ones from other enemy tribes raiding parties. Arizona's original citizens have always been survivors.

The Hopi House

The Hopis are the oldest Native American Tribe in Northern America. They are believed to have migrated from Mexico to the four-corners region of Arizona around 500 BC. After arriving in the northeastern area of Arizona, the Hopi tribe broke off into small groups and settled in different areas throughout this region. The Hopis were mainly farmers and villagers and survived as a whole do to having very limited exposure to the outside world. As their population grew, some of the smaller groups joined other bands to make a larger community on the top of mesas. When they lived in the smaller bands, their homes were in pit houses (a hole dug into the ground with a roof), but as they joined the other groups, they began to construct and live in masonry buildings (which resemble the Grand Canyon Village's Hopi House).

The Hopi Nation's belief on how they arrived in Arizona differs greatly from what we have learned in elementary and high school history books. The Hopi are direct descendants of the ancestral Pueblo Tribe, also known as the Anasazi (Ancient Ones). The name "Hopi" itself is short for *Hopituh Shi-nu-mu*, meaning "the peaceful people" or "peaceful little ones," and they are probably the most spiritual of all the Native American Tribes. It has been passed down from generation to generation that the Hopi people emerged into this world by climbing out of the underworld, which lies deep inside a small cave at the base of the Grand Canyon, right next to the Colorado River. Their tribe emerged from this other dimension, entering the Fourth World from the Third World, and they believe it is also where they will eventually enter to reach the Fifth World. Many women who are Hopi refuse to go to the bottom of the canyon because they fear evil dwells within it. Visitors to the park familiarize themselves with Native American lifestyles, cultures, and beliefs due to many of them working within the park service and living on the many reservations that surround the Grand Canyon. During the summer months, performers from the Hopi Nation put on a presentation outside the Hopi House, which sits next to the El Tovar Hotel. Their tribal stories, songs, and ceremonial dances will make your trip to the Grand Canyon complete.

The Hopi god Maasawu (maw-sow-uh) or "Skeleton Man" is also believed to come from this cave and is known as the Lord of the Dead. He is said to be responsible for teaching the Hopi the ways of agriculture, but also for warning his people about the dangers of outside influences. While Maasawu is feared by some in Hopi mythology, he is a friendly spirit who takes care of his people in the afterlife. They also believe that if you are in the canyon at night and you see a light heading towards you, it is the Skeleton Man coming to take you away with him. Around the area where their tribal ancestors emerged and the cave in which the Hopi god Maasawu lives, numerous accidents and unexplainable events are constantly occurring. The Hopi Nation will always be a big part of what we know as the Grand Canyon and its history.

Besides the Hopi, the Grand Canyon has been inhabited by several different Native American tribes throughout history. The other three primary tribes that still live near or in the canyon's depth are the Hualapai, Havasupai, and Navajo. The Havasupai Nation to this day inhabit the western portion of Grand Canyon, which is where the famous glass sky-walk is located. The Anasazi believed that the side canyon, known as *Havasu*, where the Havasupai live, has strong spirits dwelling within it. Most natives in this tribe to this day believe the inner depths of the canyon is sacred and hosts many hauntings and refuse to enter any part of it. There are also tales of visitors hearing strange and unrecognizable voices being carried in the winds while in other areas of the canyon. Many people have told stories about hearing gut-wrenching cries of pain that seem to be emanating from the beautiful, cascading blue waterfalls, and swimmers have claimed that when they are submerged under the water, they have heard disembodied voices warning them to turn around and go back towards the beaches. Although rare, certain individuals have claimed to have become possessed by the spirits of long-deceased Native Americans.

The Navajo reservation encompasses the eastern and northeastern area of the park. A Navajo legend tells that their ancestors were caught in a great flood near present-day Grand Canyon, so they had to transform themselves into fish to survive. As the flooding rose, the pressure of the rising waters broke through a canyon wall and was sent barreling down into a different side canyon saving the Navajo people. After the flooding finally came to an end, the ancestors were able to transform themselves back into humans. The side canyon that saved their lives is what we now know as the Grand Canyon.

The Navajo have their own their own unique word for a ghost, *chindi*. Death and burial rites within this culture are taken very seriously. When a loved one passes away and is not given a proper burial, their spirit becomes unable to pass through to the next life and is bound to remain on the earthly plane. The deceased's family members will be tormented by this earthbound spirit and can become afflicted with "ghost sickness." Most of the time, the surviving family members may just have a common cold, however, in their belief system, they were cursed by the vengeful spirit of the deceased.

The Navajo Nation also believe in what are known as "skinwalkers." The only people who have the power to become a skinwalker are medicine men or a witch who have the highest level of priesthood within the tribe. The legend states that to become a skinwalker, one must have committed a very evil deed, such as killing a family member. Upon doing something so evil, that person acquires powerful supernatural abilities. One of these powers is being able to mutate into any animal or human of choice and once the transformation is completed, will seek to harm or even worse, kill the living. The only sure way to stop a skinwalker is to learn who has become the cursed creature and call out their name in full. Only after their name has been spoken, the skinwalker will become very ill and could possibly die from all the evil transgressions they have committed while in their altered physical state.

In the very early 1900s, the Grand Canyon was becoming quite the popular tourist destination. Due to the sudden rise in visitation, there was a belief that the local Native American population would become eradicated from diseases and their traditional ways of life would be lost due to the increased involvement from the United States government. For the most part, the government gave the original native people of this land the worst possible lands for agriculture and survival, and those that did survive this new harsh environment would come to lose their identities as the America's Southwestern Indians and would start to blend in with Caucasian (white) settlers and their religious beliefs and clothing fashions. Promoters for the Grand Canyon started advertising to wealthy travelers to visit Native American Tribes while they were still around. The Hopi was a favorite tribe for the early tourists because of their warm hospitality. Luckily, the Santa Fe Railway decided to build the Hopi House, which sits across from the El Tovar Hotel, where tourists could interact with the Hopi people as they cooked traditional native foods and made pottery and beautiful jewelry from scratch, all the while going through their day to day ways of life.

In 1904, Mary Elizabeth Colter was asked for her architectural expertise in designing a building that would honor Native Americans. Colter was thrilled, agreed to the contract, and almost immediately envisioned how it would look once it was finished. Colter was fascinated with the construction of the original old Oraibi pueblos, which are located on the Hopi Reservation's Third Mesa in Northern Arizona. These were terraced homes with earthy designs built around the year 1150. The ancient structures are together considered the oldest continuously inhabited settlement within the country. Mary Colter hired only Hopi Native Americans to help build this enchanted building. The Hopi House opened on January 1, 1905, to the public—and everyone involved was ecstatic.

The building was specifically created to replicate a traditional adobe-style house while honoring the Hopi by including features normally found in Hopi dwellings, such as small windows, low ceilings, a ceremonial altar, and fireplaces. After the Hopi House was built, many of the native laborers, including their families, were allowed to live on the third floor (this level is now off-limits to all visitors). In the early years of the Hopi House, the new residents were kept busy making and selling beautiful homemade arts and crafts, pottery, baskets, and authentic foods to the canyon's wealthy tourists. Around the year 1930, an outdoor dance platform was installed just north of the building. Here, park visitors can enjoy viewing the Hopi dancers pay homage to their ancestors and be taught a brief history lesson about the Hopi and Navajo Nations.

As you travel around in this beautiful state, there are several locations where Native Americans can be seen along the roadsides selling precious handmade jewelry, home décor, and of course their signature fry bread. If you are interested in any of these things, make a point of stopping by the town of Cameron, which is located roughly fifty-five miles from the east entrance of the Grand Canyon. Cameron sits in the Navajo Nation Reservation at the junction of Arizona State Highway 64 and State Highway 89A. Cameron's main claim to fame (try saying that three times fast) is their legendary and historic trading post, hotel, and restaurant. Here you will find one the largest collections of authentic Native American goods in the country. My husband never passes up an opportunity to devour one their homemade Navajo tacos. Cameron Trading Post also has a few spooky tales of their own about things that go bump in the night. Trust me, the town is definitely worth a visit.

Ghostly Lore

The Hopi House remains a popular tourist destination for visitors coming to the Grand Canyon Village. Over the years, only minor maintenance has been done to this historic site, most of which has been technological, like electricity, new computer systems, climate control, and energy efficient lighting. The building remains an authentic reminder of the traditional Hopi way of life that has almost been forgotten. The main floor serves as a classy yet affordable gift store, while the second floor is an extravagant art gallery that includes hand crafted jewelry for sale. The third floor, where the Hopi people once lived, is now off limits to everyone, except for a few ghosts that like to cause some trouble after Hopi House closes for the night.

One morning, before the Hopi House opened, a sales clerk named Samantha was prepping the second floor jewelry cases for public viewing. As she approached a locked case to make sure everything was in place, she felt her heart skip a beat when she noticed that a couple of very high-priced necklaces were somehow missing. She started searching every cabinet and drawer, hoping someone accidentally set them in the wrong place, but was still unable to locate them. Samantha had been on the closing shift the night before and remembered seeing the necklaces in their proper cabinet. Her biggest worry now was how she was going to inform the Hopi House's manager, Miranda, that these very expensive necklaces were missing.

Samantha hesitantly approached the manager's office, took a deep breath and lightly knocked on the door. Miranda called out from inside the office for whoever was knocking to enter. Samantha turned the handle on the door and apprehensively stepped into the room. Miranda looked up at Samantha and clearly noticed that she seemed upset about something.

Samantha summoned all of the courage that she possibly could and told her manager that the necklaces were missing. Both women immediately went upstairs to search for them. They searched every case, cabinet, and drawer, and still came up empty-handed. The next area to be searched thoroughly was the first floor's gift shop, and once again, they could not find the expensive handmade jewelry. After all that, there was no choice but to come to the conclusion that the necklaces must have been stolen. The Hopi House is fully equipped with security cameras and alarms, but nothing was detected, so they were baffled. The question had to be asked: Was it an inside job? The next morning when the employee went upstairs, she started to do her normal routine of taking the morning inventory. In the case where the necklaces had disappeared just the day before, the missing jewelry was back in place as if they were never moved.

This seems to be a regular occurrence at the Hopi House. The blame game has been directed at to two little Hopi boys that passed away a long time ago, though nobody knows who these boys might be nor how they died. These little tykes like to send people's blood pressure off the charts. They must believe that this is their home and anything in it is theirs and fair game. These two characters can be heard giggling all around the Hopi House and can even be heard running around the second and third floors when no one living is around. Also, one needs to remember that the third floor is strictly off limits to everyone. There have been a few mornings when the Hopi House staff will walk into the building and witness dried corn spread all over the first floor. Some tourists have stated as they were walking down the stairs from the second floor that they felt as if someone was trying to forcefully push them down the stairs, and a couple of other customers have claimed that as they walked around the second floor admiring the beautiful artwork, something or someone was trying to trip them so they would fall—and they swore they could hear a child giggling that they could not see at the time they stumbled.

On certain days and hours during the spring and summer months, authentic Hopi dancers dress in extravagant clothing and dance, play wood flutes and drums, sing, and tell stories to their fascinated audience on their raised platform near the canyon's rim in front of the Hopi House. As a spectator, visitors are permitted to take pictures and videos. When the visitors finally review their pictures, several people find that they have captured the images of little Native American boys staring out of the windows from the second and third floors of the Hopi House watching the Hopi Dancers. My husband BJ and I were fortunate enough to witness this for ourselves. The two little boys only manifested when the music began and just faded away after about thirty seconds.

Strangely enough, there is always a strong gust of cool wind that blows through the trees and around the platform area just before certain songs and stories begin. This sudden burst of wind always immediately precedes the ghost children making an appearance in the windows. This phenomenon only occurs when the Hopi dancers are performing. After completing a basic investigation, it is concluded that the location of these windows are not accessible to anyone, due to the access doors being sealed shut.

Some of the dancers are quite aware they are being watched by these little boys. They have seen and felt them also. If you go into the Hopi House, enjoy looking at and purchasing the arts and crafts and all the gifts this building has to offer. Remember this was once a home to many Hopi for many generations. Maybe one day you'll be one of the lucky ones to have an paranormal experience with the lost little Hopi boys who think the Hopi House is still their home.

Chapter 9

VERKAMP'S VISITOR CENTER

Verkamp's Visitor Center is another historic building that neighbors the Hopi House to the east, built by John George Verkamp. Verkamp was born in Cincinnati, Ohio, on February 22, 1877. While growing up in Cincinnati, John's childhood friends were the Babbitt brothers (there were five of them) who lived across the street from him and his family. The Babbitt brothers had always dreamt of eventually owning a large cattle ranch in the wild west, so when the brothers finally pooled all their money together (twenty thousand dollars), two of the brothers (Billy and Dave) agreed to head out west to scout for prime cattle grazing land. After the two brothers found the perfect setting to establish a cattle ranch east of Flagstaff, Arizona, the other three Babbitt brothers (George, Charlie, and Edward) arrived, with John Verkamp accompanying them. The Babbitts also successfully opened up a mercantile store in Flagstaff.

By 1898, John Verkamp had hopes of possibly opening up his own store on the Grand Canyon's South Rim after hearing about all the visitors flocking to see this huge hole in the ground. He took a wagon-load of Native American blankets to the canyon to sell for the Babbitt brothers and was fortunate to meet Martin Bugguln, owner of the Bright Angel Hotel. John Verkamp explained to Mr. Bugguln about his plan of owning and operating the first curio store at the canyon and Bugguln offered Verkamp one of the Bright Angel tents to help begin his business. Within a few short weeks after opening up shop, John was unfortunately unable to make enough profit to keep the tent open, so he sadly had to give up on his investment and promptly returned to Ohio.

The water pump in front of
Verkamp's Visitor Center, circa 2007

By 1905, tourism to the South Rim increased drastically, thanks to the new Santa Fe Railway, which traveled to the Grand Canyon

Village and the grand opening of the luxurious El Tovar Hotel. John Verkamp had not completely given up on becoming a successful merchant at the canyon; he was just waiting for the right time financially to return and now saw an opportunity to achieve his dream. In 1906, John proudly opened the newest business venture in the main village and named it "Verkamp's Curios." This time instead of being inside a tent, Mr. Verkamp built a two-story, wood-shingled building roughly one hundred feet from the canyon's rim east of the El Tovar Hotel and Hopi House. The second floor would serve as his home, where as the first floor would have plenty of room to eventually become a successful curio store. John Verkamp also came up with an inventive way to collect rain water and melted snow run-off, which is a precious commodity in such a harsh, arid region. He designed the roof of his home/ business to capture any moisture that fell on the roof and it drain into a cistern (storage tank) underneath the front porch that had a pump, which enabled him to use reservoir of water whenever he needed it.

The new Verkamp's Curio Store sold Native American art and crafts, post cards, and various other types of souvenirs that were affordable to all tourists. Placed out on the front porch was a large iron meteorite that John had acquired from a friend. On more than one occasion, thieves had tried to steal it, but were always unsuccessful. During one evening, after Mr. Verkamp had gone to bed, some pranksters rolled this giant hunk of iron to block the entry into the front and only doors, forcing John to find an alternative way out of the building.

Even though John Verkamp had become a successful businessman within the Grand Canyon Village, he still spent the majority of his time in Flagstaff. Three of his sisters had moved to Arizona and married three of the Babbitt brothers. While spending time with his family in Flagstaff, John met a woman named Catherine Wolfe, who had recently moved to Arizona to live with her brothers, who were working for the railway. They soon fell in love and were married in 1912. After the wedding, Catherine continued to reside in Flagstaff and the newlyweds were blessed with four children: Margaret (Peggy), John George Jr. (Jack), Mary Janet (Jan), and Catherine (Katie).

On October 29, 1929—Black Thursday—the Roaring Twenties came to an abrupt end as the United States of America officially entered into one of its darkest eras: the Great Depression. Family vacations and traveling during this difficult time had basically become nonexistent. Every national park around the country suffered financially. All the businesses around the Grand Canyon's Village began to deteriorate. John Verkamp's business was not immune to the crumbling economy, which meant that he could no longer afford for his family to live in two separate households. In 1936, Catherine Verkamp and their four children packed all of their belongings and moved to the Grand Canyon, into their new home above the store. The whole family pitched in to help keep the store up and running during the final years of the Depression. After the United States finally got back on track, Catherine and the children continued to reside at the canyon. The Grand Canyon National Park Service began hiring full-time employees and offered housing to those who brought their families with them. The Grand Canyon Village now saw an increase in school-aged children that needed a proper education. John and Catherine Verkamp were instrumental in establishing a full-time school that taught kindergarten through the twelfth grade. The Grand Canyon is the only national park that has a permanent unified school district. This husband-and-wife team also established chapters of the Boy Scouts and Girl Scouts for the younger children living in the village.

John George Verkamp passed away on April 4, 1944, from a stroke. After his untimely death, Catherine and their children continued making the Verkamp's Curios store a popular destination choice for visiting tourists. On April 4, 1979, thirty-five years to the day of her husband's passing, Catherine Verkamp joined her husband on the other side. John and Catherine are both buried next to each other in a family plot, along with nine other family members, inside the Pioneer Cemetery. In 2008, the surviving family members decided they were not going to renew their contract with the National Park Service to keep the curio shop open. The park service immediately took possession of the Verkamp's Curio store and turned it into a Visitor Center. The Verkamp's Visitor Center is now on the National Register of Historic Places. The only problem is someone forgot to tell the spirits of the Verkamp family, that the building is no longer their home.

Ghostly Lore

Nobody is really sure just who or how many spirits call Verkamp's Visitor Center home. Strange sounds reverberate inside the building well after closing time, and a female ghost has been spotted multiple times on the second floor where the Verkamp family lived. The parking lot adjacent to Verkamp's Visitor Center is reported to have an unfriendly spirit that seems to enjoy scaring anyone walking through it during the nighttime hours.

National Park Service employees will usually not divulge any information about paranormal experiences they've had to the general public. Whether they are scared of being ridiculed or being fired, it's hard to get them to open up about the existence of ghosts. I was lucky enough to have an employee that had worked there, Melissa, tell me some stories she had heard from fellow co-workers and what she's personally witnessed during her employment at Verkamp's. Melissa said that many co-workers hear muffled disembodied voices when in the building after it is closed. Several people have heard their name being called by a male's voice when they are alone in the building. Dark shadows are often seen moving around on the first and second floors. When workers are finishing up their closing duties on the first floor, they can distinctly hear footsteps of someone walking around on the second floor. When they go upstairs to check to see who is there, they discover they are all alone. Well, sort of …

If that isn't bad enough, the parking lot adjacent to Verkamp's Visitor Center is reported to have a malicious entity that stalks and terrorizes anyone who happens to be walking through the lot late at night. A terrifying encounter with this entity happened one evening to El Tovar dinner server Pam. She had gone into Flagstaff earlier that day to do some personal shopping to get her through for the next couple of busy weeks. By the time she returned back to the canyon, she realized she was running late for work. Pam took a quick shower and jumped into her car and sped towards the El Tovar. Normally, she would park her car by the Grand Canyon's mule barn and railroad tracks and walk the rest of the way to her job. This day, Pam needed to find a closer parking spot, so she wouldn't get into trouble for being late for work, having already been talked to a couple of times before for being tardy. As she approached the village area, she decided she had no choice but to park in the El Tovar Hotel's parking lot that's technically reserved for visitors. As soon as Pam reached the top of the hill and turned right into the car parking area, she was overly thrilled to see someone backing out of a spot at the end of the road next to Verkamp's Visitors Center and claimed the spot.

It had been a long, busy night inside the restaurant, far more hectic than normal. There had been multiple large parties that evening and diners for some reason seemed to be extremely rude and overly needy. Pam was closing that night, so she was one of the last servers to leave the restaurant. It was a little after midnight when she exited through the front door of the lodge to walk to her car. As she started walking across the roundabout in front of the Hopi House, she noticed the moon wasn't visible and the parking lot she had to walk through to get to her car was pitch black.

Pam was all alone and didn't see anyone else out walking around. Cautiously, she began to walk through an endless sea of cars, scanning from side to side with each car she passed, keeping a watchful eye out for any possible threat that might have come her way. That's when she noticed a solid black human-shaped figure near the end of the parking lot close to Verkamp's Visitor Center. Even though it was totally dark out, she could still distinctly see that this person was slowly walking between cars, but it seemed more like it was floating, not taking steps. Pam felt her heart in her throat and began shaking. She considered turning around and running back to the El Tovar but right in front of her eyes, she saw this thing just fade away. She finally spotted her car and ran to it as fast as she could, got in, and locked the doors. She was trembling uncontrollably, so she tried to regain her composure before attempting to drive her car.

When she placed her keys into the ignition and was about ready to start the car, she glanced up at the second floor of the Verkamp's Visitor Center because she noticed an eerie, luminous light in a window. Pam knew the building had closed at dusk and no one was supposed to be inside at that time of night. She continued to watch the window that was emitting the light and said that it eventually resembled a flame that would burn in an old-fashioned hurricane lamp. Then, to her horror, Pam saw an old woman with a blue glow around her peer out quickly from the window. Pam realized that this woman wasn't alive and what she was actually seeing must have been a ghost. She backed her car up quickly and drove home as fast as she could. Pam had told several people about what she experienced that night and discovered that she was not alone in encountering the paranormal realm near the parking lot next to the Verkamp's Visitor Center.

Park employee Charlie has always been considered a dedicated and exceptional worker for many years. When he first arrived at the Grand Canyon to begin his job, Charlie began to hear almost immediately about the different ghost stories that allegedly occur inside the park from other staff members. Charlie was actually hoping that he would experience something ghostly for himself. He already had a strong belief in ghosts and hauntings, having had lived in a haunted apartment complex in his hometown of Peachtree City, Georgia. Several years had gone by and Charlie had not witnessed anything paranormal for himself at the canyon, until a night in April 2012, when his supernatural dry spell came to an abrupt end.

Charlie had been working at the El Tovar's front desk as a guest service agent. It was around 11:00 p.m., when he was finally able to call it quits for the day and go home. He was walking through the lobby when someone called out his name from behind him. He turned around and saw one of his good friends—Stephanie, a bartender from the El Tovar Cocktail Lounge who was a member of the Hopi Tribe—also leaving for the night. Charlie decided to escort Stephanie to her car. Stephanie could only find one parking spot when she had arrived at work and that was next to the Verkamp's Visitor Center. Because of the late hour and cold weather that had enveloped the canyon that evening, Charlie and Stephanie were the only people walking around outside.

As they slowly strolled passed the Hopi House, Charlie was able to see a dark figure walking towards them from the parking lot area close to Verkamp's building. Figuring that someone was coming back from a cold walk, Charlie asked Stephanie if she could see a person walking towards them. She said she could see someone but had an eerie feeling about it. She had also mentioned to Charlie that the person seemed as if it was gliding on air and not actually walking on solid ground. When the figure got within fifteen feet of them, they both noticed that this person wasn't wearing a jacket, which was unusual given the temperature outside being a brisk twenty-five degrees Fahrenheit. As the two were within mere feet of the stranger, Charlie and Stephanie politely said, "Hello, how are you?" As they waited for a response from the person, the figure disappeared right before their eyes. Stephanie instinctively let out a scream while Charlie grabbed her arm and they rushed towards her car. They quickly stumbled in and sped away. Due to Stephanie's mystical upbringing, she drove straight to the Hopi Reservation after she dropped Charlie off at his home where she could receive a spiritual cleansing. Charlie on the other hand was ecstatic about finally being able to witness one of the Grand Canyon Village's ghosts with his own two eyes.

Verkamp's Visitor Center has had its ups and downs and also had a loving family reside inside it for almost one hundred years. It's an awesome building to go into and browse through its history. Just be aware that there is a good possibility that the building's history just might be watching you and every move you make.

Chapter 10
LOOKOUT STUDIO

Precariously perched on the edge of a dizzying cliff at an elevation of over seven thousand feet stands the Lookout Studio. This popular structure lies only a few steps west of the Bright Angel Lodge and offers unobstructed views of the canyon as well as a sheer 300-foot drop just below its foundation. This beautiful building is yet another masterpiece designed by architect Mary Elizabeth Colter who, as we know, loved the Native American lifestyle, culture, and dwellings (of course). Having been constructed in 1914 using native stone and wood, the Lookout Studio was designed to resemble a traditional southwestern structure from a forgotten era and was expertly constructed to blend in seamlessly with the rugged environment surrounding it.

Viewing the South Rim from the North Rim, roughly ten aerial miles away, Lookout Studio blends in perfectly as just part of the top rock layer of the South Rim, just like the Thunderbird and Kachina Lodges. On the inside of the studio are multiple floor levels with a fireplace. Multiple windows are also featured in the building for better viewing of the canyon even when it gets crowded. For the tourists with strong stomachs and no severe pho-bia of heights, there are several outdoor balconies on different lev-els for closer viewing of the inner canyon. These balconies also contain high-powered telescopes that visitors can use to watch hikers going up and down the Bright Angel Trail, observe wildlife such as Big Horn Sheep that live on the canyon's rocky cliffs, wit-ness the innermost beauty of the canyon that you can't see with the naked eye and to view the endangered California condors that are nesting carefully in the walls of the canyon.

However, what most people don't know is that the Lookout Studio was built mainly as a way to sabotage another popular tourist destination that was competing for business against the Fred Harvey Company in the early 1900s. It was no secret that the Kolb Brothers and the Fred Harvey Company had a bitter resent-ment towards each other. The Kolb Brothers owned a successful photography studio and gift shop at the beginning of the Bright Angel Trailhead. Emery and Ellsworth Kolb had already been liv-ing happily at the Grand Canyon for over a decade and their pho-tography studio, (which doubled as their home) was only about one hundred feet farther west down the Rim Trail from where the new Lookout Studio was built.

The Fred Harvey Company wanted to put their primary com-petitors, the Kolb Brothers, permanently out of business, so they devised a plan to build a gift store and observation deck closer to the main lodges that would cause a bottleneck and obstruct visi-tor traffic towards the Kolb Brothers studio. The exact location of Lookout Studio was purposely built as a strategic, master ruse to deceive the canyon's early years tourist into thinking that they had entered into the Kolb Studio which was in all actuality the new Lookout Studio. This plan worked for a while as many visitors that went into the Lookout Studio instantly assumed that this was the last gift store in the village and didn't venture any farther west. The general public finally realized that the Lookout Studio was a ploy and that the beloved Kolb Studio was still a short walk down the trail. Even though the Lookout Studio was first built as a cut-throat business solution to combat a rival, it is still a very popular tourist destination to this day.

On May 28, 1987, the Lookout Studio was placed on the National Register of Historic Places. The gift shop carries a wide assortment of souvenirs ranging from native jewelry to southwestern décor to clothing and books. Trying to get close to the outside balconies to see all the different views can be quite challenging by side-stepping sometimes less than friendly tourists trying to negotiate through the pedestrian-jammed patios.

Every building in the village holds dark secrets and the Lookout Studio is no exception. Since it rests on a steep cliff, some individuals have chosen this site to sadly end their lives. The stone walls that encompasses the outside balcony were supposed to protect visitors viewing the depths of the canyon from accidentally falling to their deaths.

Ghostly Lore

Over sixty years ago, a former employee of Fred Harvey Company who was living in Phoenix, Arizona, came to the canyon to end his life. He wrote a suicide note, left it in his room in the Bright Angel Lodge, walked to the cliffs next to the Lookout Studio, and jumped 150 feet to his death.

In recent years, a young man went to the Lookout Studio and walked out onto one of the multilevel balconies, and in front of many witnesses, he stepped up on the retaining wall and plummeted

250 feet to his death. As morbid as it may sound, the Lookout Studio has unfortunately become the perfect setting for producing ghosts. Since the Lookout Studio sits directly on a cliff, it is one of the first buildings to close its doors just before dusk or during inclement weather like snow, ice, or strong winds due to its close proximity to deadly drop-offs. When the store finally does close for the day, the staff can begin to clean up after the customers. The main door of Lookout Studio is equipped with electronic theft detectors. On more than a few occasions, those detectors have gone off for no apparent reason, startling the employees that are left inside the building. There doesn't seem to be a logical explanation for this malfunction, as the equipment is routinely inspected and are in perfect working order. Could ghosts be looking for souvenir t-shirts or too warm by a fire on the cold canyon nights? Who knows? Maybe… Several long-tenured employees believe that the building has a resident ghost. Footsteps are commonly heard walking around on the stone floors and merchandise has been seen moving around by unseen hands.

A few years ago, Lily, an employee from Bright Angel Lodge clocked out of work at 9:30 p.m. Lily's boyfriend, Jake, also worked at the park. One night Jake showed up at the Bright Angel front desk to pick up Lily when she got off of work. After Lily clocked out, Jake decided to escort her out onto to the rim because the night sky that evening was crystal clear, and the stars were brightly sparkling. Jake thought how romantic it would be to sit with Lily on the rim's wall and just stargaze. They exited out the Bright Angel Lodge's back doors, which lead them directly towards the canyon's rim. Jake decided to move farther west down the trail to get away from the outside lights that the Bright Angel's Lodge was giving off so they could have a better view of the sky.

As they strolled in front of Lookout Studio, Lily noticed movement inside the store. The store had been closed for a few hours and was completely dark inside except for a very faint light emanating from a display case. All of a sudden, the light from the case was blocked out by someone or something that was walking around in the store. Lily and Jake watched for about a minute as something kept blocking out the light by walking in front of it. As this suspicious activity was occurring, a mutual friend of theirs walked up to them. This friend, Alex, was from the park's security team and was out on his nightly patrol. Alex asked the couple what they were up to and Lily told him she believed that maybe someone had broken into the Lookout Studio, that they were seeing some kind of movement roaming around inside the building. Lily, Jake, and Alex walked towards the front door of the store. The front door was secure, so Alex took out his flashlight and shined the powerful beam through the front window which illuminated most of the gift shop. Everything appeared to be in its proper place and there was no sign that someone had broken in. Confused, they walked back to the Rim Trail. Alex had to continue on with his patrol, so the group parted ways.

Lily and Jake knew that they had seen someone or something walking around inside the Lookout Studio. They had a feeling that what they saw might have been a ghost, because both of them had heard rumors about odd things happening within the Lookout Studio and also its outside balconies. The two lovebirds decided jointly to turn their romantic stargazing into hard-nosed detective work in search of the paranormal. After about an hour of not seeing anything else out of the ordinary inside the building, Jake told Lily that the stake-out was a bust and time to call it a night. As they began to walk back towards the Bright Angel Lodge, Lily glanced back at the Lookout Studio, and as if on cue, she once again saw the figure walking around the gift shop, blocking out the cabinets light. However, when Lily told Jake it was back, Jake told her that he was still leaving that the ghost had already made a fool out of him once that night, it wasn't going to happen twice. The couple went home with more questions than answers. The next day when Lily was at work, she saw one of her friends that was a manager at the Lookout Studio. Lily told her manager friend what she witnessed the night before. The manager wasn't surprised at all, she just smiled and said, "That happens all the time. We just don't tell anyone because we don't want to be considered nuts."

Another ghostly sighting that has occurred at the Lookout Studio on a few occasions deals with the outside balconies. Several people who were out on the balconies have seen a male ghostly figure climb up onto the wall and fall into the canyon. All of the witnesses have described the same scene. The man is transparent, with brown hair, small stature, and wearing blue jeans, but he never makes a sound. This is what is known as a residual haunting, which is something that has already happened in the past. In most cases, in this kind of haunting, there is no actual ghost. When a lot of emotional or traumatic events take place, the surrounding environment can somehow record the incident and when conditions are right can play back the scene to the unsuspecting audience. This is the simplest way for me to explain that to those who don't fully understand how the paranormal world works. Don't feel too bad because even the more experienced investigators sometimes don't fully understand and if they claim they know everything about the paranormal world, they are in denial and are sadly mistaken.

Chapter 11

KOLB STUDIO

Brothers Ellsworth and Emery Kolb were as much an integral part of the Grand Canyon as the Colorado River itself. No living person today will ever discover all the wonders, magic, and mysteries this canyon is concealing, but the Kolb Brothers possibly came the closest to uncovering all the canyon's hidden secrets.

Ellsworth was born on January 4, 1876, in Springfield, Pennsylvania, to Minister Edward Kolb and his wife, Ella. Five years later, on February 15, 1881, the Kolb family was blessed with another son, Emery. Ellsworth and Emery also shared their childhood with two more brothers and an adopted sister. Ellsworth and Emery were boys through and through and liked a good adventure and scare. In May of 1889, a torrential rainstorm swamped the area around their home in Springfield. Rivers and creeks were overflowing their banks and when terrified homeowners were fleeing for higher grounds, Ellsworth and Emery saw a potential to become pirates and sail the high seas. The two brothers built a wooden raft to try to navigate the high waters, but mind you neither of the boys could swim. As the raging flood waters swelled even higher and was littered with fallen trees and debris, the young pirates' shoddy raft started to break apart. Quickly thinking, Ellsworth grabbed both ends of the wooden raft with his feet and hands to keep his brother and himself from perishing. Ellsworth was able to get what was left of the broken raft and his terrified brother to dry ground without either boy containing any serious injuries.

When Ellsworth became a teenager, he held different jobs to bring in money to help support his parents and siblings. When he turned twenty-four, Ellsworth decided it was time for him to start his own life so he headed out west. He lived in several states including Colorado and California and became a jack of all trades. While Ellsworth was in California, he met some men who convinced him to join them on a ship bound for the Orient and his passage would be free if he signed on as a member of the crew. A day before he was set to sail to Asia, Ellsworth saw an advertisement saying "Come to the Grand Canyon" and he believed the article was specifically meant for him. The next day, with very little money left in his pockets, Ellsworth packed what little belongings he had left and headed off towards Arizona. When he finally reached the Grand Canyon, he was flat broke. Luckily, Ellsworth met Martin Bugguln, who owned the Bright Angel Hotel and Tent Cabins, almost immediately upon his arrival and Bugguln was in need of a maintenance man, so he hired Ellsworth on the spot.

Back home in Pennsylvania, Emery had found a new passion in the form of photography—so much so that he saved up enough money from his side jobs to purchase a small camera. He loved taking pictures of anything that caught his attention and was so uniquely talented with it that he was able to make some extra money by selling some of his photos to the town folk. After some time, Ellsworth was able to save up enough money working for

Martin Bugguln that he was able take a trip back home to Pennsylvania to visit his family.

While on his visit, he convinced Emery to relocate to the Grand Canyon with him. Their parents on the other hand were not too thrilled with the idea of Emery leaving without some kind of employment. Ellsworth said he would return back to the canyon and find a job that would be suitable for Emery. In October 1902, Emery received a letter from Ellsworth saying he had found a job for him working at the Hance Mine at the canyon and also a train ticket. Almost immediately, Emery was on a train that departed from Pittsburg, Pennsylvania, and his final stop was going to be in Williams, Arizona.

Emery already knew he wanted to become a professional photographer, and after hearing all the stories from Ellsworth about the Grand Canyon, he knew that's where he would make it rich. After he arrived in Williams, he walked around the old west town until he came across a photography shop operated by a man named Mr. Arbogast. He spoke to Emery for a short while and informed him that his store was for sale. This opportunity greatly intrigued Emery, so he told Mr. Arbogast that when he eventually made it to the canyon, he would talk to his brother and see what he thought about the possibility of purchasing the store. Later that day, when Emery finally arrived at the Grand Canyon, he discovered that the Hance Asbestos Mine had permanently closed and he was out of a job. He told Ellsworth about the photography store in Williams, but he claimed that he didn't have any money to purchase it. The next day, Ellsworth boarded the train to Williams to talk to Mr. Arbogast about the store. Emery had remained at the canyon and helped Martin Bugguln out where he could. When

Ellsworth returned later that day, he was ecstatic to tell his brother that they were the proud new owners of the photography store.

Emery moved to Williams for a short time while he ran the store, but his heart still yearned for the Grand Canyon. The two brothers discussed opening up a photography studio near the rim, but Ellsworth's employer Martin Bugguln did everything he could to sabotage their plans. Unfortunately for Bugguln, the Kolb brothers found a guardian angel in Ralph Cameron. If you remember correctly from the Bright Angel Lodge chapter, Cameron owned the area around the Bright Angel Trailhead. He gave the brothers land to open up their own photography studio. Bugguln and the railroad fought hard to keep the Kolb brothers from going into business, claiming that their studio would hurt Bugguln and the Santa Fe Railway's souvenir sales, but when all was said and done, Ellsworth and Emery were granted permission to start their new business at the head of the Bright Angel Trailhead.

The brothers realized that starting a photography studio at the Grand Canyon was going to be difficult, however Ellsworth and Emery proved to everyone that where there's a will, there's a way. Their studio started out as a crude tent. The tent let in too much light, so finding a suitable darkroom to develop the negatives of the pictures they were going to take was critical. Emery came up with the best solution. Below the rim were several abandoned mines, and some went far enough back to block out all of the sunlight.

The next road block was that Emery would need an ample supply of fresh water for the development of the pictures. The Grand Canyon's Southern Rim to this day does not have its own water supply. It needs to be imported in by a pipeline from the North Rim, around eighteen miles away. The water source on the

South Rim of the canyon back in the early 1900s was brought in daily by the train. Emery knew exactly what he had to do. The closest water source to the South Rim from the head of the Bright Angel Trailhead was 4.6 miles one way down into the canyon at the Indian Garden Campground. Here he would be supplied with enough water for the development of the photos. Emery ran this trail several times a day to make his business a success, and a success it was. Every morning the brothers would meet the cautiously optimistic tourists riding the mule train down the Bright Angel Trail into the depths of the canyon. They would take photos of the riders on their reliable, sure-footed, and smelly mode of transportation, and after the mule train departed down the trail, Emery would always follow to get fresh water so the pictures would be developed and ready for sale when the mule riders arrived back later in the day.

In 1903 the brothers started construction on a permanent resident/business near the head of the Bright Angel Trail. The structure began as a small studio on a ledge next to a sheer drop into the canyon. As time went on and after the brothers made more money, they would add more rooms onto the studio. Ellsworth and Emery hiked and learned as much about the canyon and its topography as they could by going into the canyon as often as possible and taking photographs of areas deep within the abyss that had only been previously seen by the canyon's ancient tribes.

In 1905, Emery had met, fell in love with, and married a young lady by the name of Blanche Bender. As soon as they were wed, she moved into the small house/studio with Emery and Ellsworth. By 1908, the newlyweds were blessed with the birth of a daughter they named Edith. Besides caring for her new daughter, Blanche also helped the brothers with their business by running the gift shop, handling the bookkeeping, and occasionally helping with the photography development.

In 1910, Ellsworth and Emery decided they were going to do something that no person before them had ever done. They were going to buy a Pathé brand movie camera and run the Colorado River by boat through the Grand Canyon, recording the trip on film. They started their journey in 1911 and it ended in the early winter of 1912. They traveled the river in two custom-made boats that had been constructed in Wisconsin by the Racine Boat Company. This was considered a historical event and they even received attention from Hollywood film producer Cecil B. DeMille, who printed the movie for the now famous, Grand Canyon's own, Kolb Brothers. The siblings added a theater to their expanding home/ studio, and beginning in 1915, the movie was shown continuously every day for the massive droves of tourists. Due to it having been a silent movie, a narration was performed at all showing by Emery himself up until 1932. This movie was so popular with the Grand Canyon tourists that it was shown for sixty-one years at an estimate of over fifty thousand times until Emery's death in 1976. This well-documented homemade film by two adventurous brothers is said to be the longest running film in the history of the world.

By 1911, the Fred Harvey Company had done everything they could to have Emery and Ellsworth close the photography studios doors. The brothers were not going to leave their home and place of business. The Fred Harvey Company and Santa Fe Railway had the Lookout Studio built purposely in front of the Kolb Studio to take business away from them. This plan didn't work, and the Fred Harvey Company finally gave up trying to destroy the Kolb Brothers' life dream.

As with all siblings, the Kolb brothers had a disagreement, and a certain falling out would make Ellsworth say his goodbyes to the Grand Canyon and head west to make a new life in Los Angeles California, even though he would return occasionally to the canyon to visit his brother. A financial agreement was eventually reached that Emery would send Ellsworth $150.00 every month until Ellsworth's passing in 1960. Emery continued building onto the Kolb Studio until it reached five stories tall and contained an astounding twenty-three rooms.

In 1963, Emery sold the Kolb Studio to the National Park Service for $65,000 on the condition that he and his family could continue to live and work there until his passing. Emery passed away on December 11, 1976. He is buried next to his loving and faithful wife Blanche, and their daughter Edith's grave is near her parents within the Pioneer Cemetery. Ellsworth was also interred within the Pioneer Cemetery. The Kolb Studio is now run by the Grand Canyon Association. Most of the studio is off limits to visitors. There is still a gift store and guest are permitted to walk down the stairs to the auditorium where there is a little museum in honor of the Kolb Brothers and where you can still enjoy watching Ellsworth and Emery's movie as they journeyed down the Colorado River. This fascinating building is on the National Register of Historic Places list, plus it seems to have a few ghosts residing in it.

Ghostly Lore

A couple of months after Emery Kolb passed away, his grandson Emery Lehnert was going through some of his grandfather's personal belongings that were left behind in the garage of the studio. Inside a canvas boat that was perched up in the rafters, grandson Emery discovered a human skeleton with a bullet hole in the skull bundled up inside the boat. Rumors were running rampant as to why Emery Kolb was hiding a human skeleton. There are two competing theories as to whom the remains might belong. The first theory continues to remain an unsolved mystery. In 1928, newlyweds Glen and Bessie Hyde were hoping to achieve world-wide fame by becoming the first man and woman team to success-fully raft the Colorado River through the Grand Canyon. Bessie would have also become the first woman to ever run and survive the river's deadly rapids through the canyon. Unfortunately, the Hydes disappeared forever while traveling the river through the Grand Canyon.

In 1927, Bessie Louise Haley had been living and attending school in San Francisco, California, and shared an apartment with an aspiring model and actress Eraine Granstedt. Bessie, a petite and pretty girl, was originally from Parkersburg, West Virginia, but at nineteen years of age, she married her high school sweet-heart and resided with him temporarily in Kentucky. Their mar-riage sadly lasted only two months. After the separation, Bessie felt compelled to move to California and attend the California School of Fine Arts. Bessie and Eraine one day decided to board a ship in San Francisco that was heading to Los Angeles. For Eraine, heading to Los Angeles meant riches and fame for her. Here she would become an actress, but it was not clear why Bessie wanted to travel there.

Glen Hyde, a handsome and adventurous man, was visiting California and was also aboard the ship. During the voyage to Los Angeles, Glen and Bessie met and fell in love. The two became inseparable and when it was time for Glen to return home to Mur-taugh, Idaho, Bessie went with him. A little over a year later and after her divorce from her high school sweetheart was finalized,

Glen and Bessie were pronounced husband and wife on April 28, 1928, and resided on the Hyde family farm.

When Glen and Bessie married, it was at the beginning of the Hyde farm's busy season and the honeymoon was going to have to wait until after the fall harvest. Glen, being the adventurer he was, wanted to do something special for their honeymoon that no other husband and wife had ever done before. Glen discussed his plan with Bessie that only the two of them would raft the Colorado River through the Grand Canyon and document their journey. The first husband and wife team to ever navigate the Colorado River through the Grand Canyon's deadly rapids would have to become headline news. He believed that they would become rich and famous if they wrote a book about their experience, and Hollywood would hear about their adventure and make a movie about their story.

Glen was personally involved in constructing a boat known as a sweep scow, which he was well experienced at piloting, for him and his new wife's journey down the Colorado River. This kind of a boat resembles a huge horse trough. It was twenty feet long, five feet wide, and three feet deep, and the pilot used an oar that stretched out of the bow and stern—not the kind of boat someone would want to take over ominous rapids. On October 28, 1928, the honeymooners set off in their newly constructed sweep scow from Green River, Utah. The boat was stocked with food and provisions, a rifle, and mattresses to sleep on. Glen, however, refused to put any kind of life preservers on the boat. Glen had an ego and said he could handle anything the Colorado River would throw at him and his bride. If everything went as planned, their journey would end on December 9, 1928 in Needles, California, where Glen's father would be waiting for the couple.

Things seemed to be going well at first for the newlyweds. By November 7, the adventurers reached Lees Ferry on the Colorado River. This is where Glen Canyon, which is mostly located in Utah, ends and the Grand Canyon officially begins. Things quickly began to turn dicey, when Glen and Bessie reached an area known as Marble Canyon. At this point of their doomed adventure, they were besieged with seemingly endless areas of violent white-water rapids that were just relentless on their physical assaults on the Hydes. One set of rapids were so harrowing, they knocked Glen into the freezing white water, but Bessie somehow found the strength to drag him back into the boat.

Glen didn't seem fazed by this almost deadly encounter with the river rapids, but it was obvious that Bessie was terrified for their lives. The next day the two exhausted newlyweds made their way to the beach that connected them to the South Kaibab Trail. Having become depleted of some necessary supplies, the weary couple hiked up the steep trail towards the Grand Canyon Village. Once at the top, they were recognized by many people as the first couple trying to navigate the Colorado River through the Grand Canyons deadly depths. Glen was getting a taste of fame by being acknowledged as a celebrity. Emery Kolb happened to be in the crowd of adoring fans and introduced himself to the Hydes. He opened up his home to Glen and Bessie so they could rest. Here, Emery offered Glen his own personal life jackets for them to use. Emery knew just how dangerous the upcoming rapids were and expressed to Glen that what was coming was possibly the most deadly part of their whole journey and they probably would not survive without any form of a life preserver. Glen flat out turned Emery down, saying they didn't need any artificial aid. Emery pleaded with Glen to at least buy an inner tube or two, which angered the egotistical boatman. Glen claimed they were going to finish the trip the way they started, with no assistance from anyone or anything. Bessie on the other hand was now a frail, tattered woman from what she used to be. It was obvious she wanted nothing more than for this journey to come to an end. There was no excitement or thrill left in her eyes. She did not care about fame and riches, and the only reason she continued with the trip was because Glen demanded she did.

Glen realized they were short on money when it came time to buy their desperately needed items that they had ran out of. A businessman from San Francisco named Adolph Sutro was visiting the park at the time that Glen and Bessie ascended the trail from the abyss. Adolph made a deal with Glen that he would furnish them with two weeks' worth of food if he could hitch a ride with them on their boat roughly seven miles to Hermit Rapids. The stipulation would be that they would receive the groceries by his partners only after he was dropped off at the arranged designated spot. Glen agreed, and after they had a little bit of rest they headed back down the South Kaibab Trail towards the river. Bessie had become friends with Emery's daughter, Edith, in their short stay. As they walked towards the trailhead, Bessie looked down at Edith's shoes and said, "I wonder if I shall ever wear pretty shoes again?" Edith had informed her father, Emery, about Bessie's troubling statement. Emery was outraged with Glen. Emery knew they would not survive the upcoming rapids without any kind of life preservers. Emery had fallen into the river a couple of times himself and almost didn't make it out alive and he was wearing a life preserver.

The last time Glen and Bessie Hyde were ever seen alive again was on November 18, 1928. On this date, Glen dropped off Adolph

Sutro at the agreed spot on Hermit Rapids, and as promised, there was food waiting for Glen and Bessie on the banks. Mr. Sutro and some men claimed that Bessie also tried to leave the boat at that time, fearing for her life. But Glen physically picked her up and placed her back in the boat. On December 6, Glen's father, Rollin C. Hyde was waiting in Needles, California, for his son and new daughter-in-law's adventure to come to an end. When they didn't arrive, Mr. Hyde assumed the honeymooners were just running late on their trip. By December 16, with still no sighting of Glen or Bessie, Mr. Hyde contacted as many possible agencies to help in the aide of finding his missing family. On December 19, a search plane spotted a scow like the one Glen and Bessie were on floating in an eddy at river mile 237. A land search crew was dispatched to the area, which included Emery and Ellsworth Kolb. The boat and all of Glen and Bessie's provisions were still pretty much intact, but the couple were never seen again. There was a journal on the boat that belonged to Bessie that was in good shape. However, there was nothing in it to help the search party find the lost couple or their fate.

The disappearance of the Hydes is considered an unsolved mystery even to this day. What happened to the two honeymooners? Did they drown? Did they run into trouble and had to hike out from the canyon's floor? Once the skeleton was found in Emery Kolb's garage hanging high in the rafters, many people speculated that Glen Hyde met his death not by the hands of the deadly Colorado River, but by Emery Kolb's hands himself. The theory is that Emery was so outraged by Glens dismissal of Bessie's life that Mr. Kolb took things into his own hands. It's believed by some that Emery, knowing the canyon better than most, hiked down to the river in a secret spot known only by him to meet the couple and beg Glen to consider Bessie feelings and either end the trip or use life preservers.

Things got out of hand between the two men, which resorted in Glen's death. Emery then took Glen's remains to his studio and hid the body from the rest of the world. Bessie then supposedly took on a new identity and began a new life. A woman years later was on a river rafting trip through the Colorado River. Her name was Georgie White Clarke and claimed she was, in actuality, Bessie Hyde. This woman knew a lot about Bessie's life before her supposed death and Georgie also had some resemblance to the late Mrs. Hyde. Critics, of course blasted Ms. Clarke's allegations and she was considered a liar. Even on her death bed in 1992, Georgie White Clarke never wavered about actually being Bessie Hyde. After her passing, actual items that belonged to Glen and Bessie Hyde were found among Ms. Clarke's possessions. Now mind you that this story is far-fetched and a medical examiner, after a careful examination of the skeleton, cleared Emery Kolb of any wrongdoing, claiming that the skeleton was much older than Glen Hyde would have been and also smaller in size. There are still some, though, who believe that regardless of this evidence the skeleton is still the remains of Glen Hyde.

The second possible theory about the skeleton's true identity boils down to it being an old prospector that was looking for gold and silver inside the canyon walls back in the 1800s and had committed suicide many years before the remains were found in sand and rocks. Either way, having any human remains without a proper burial on anyone's property gives ripe condition for a haunting.

When the Grand Canyon Association took over the Kolb Studio, a few employees started noticing strange things occurring within the building that were unexplainable. When employees arrive for work in the mornings, books will be scattered across the floor in the gift shop. Some books have been discovered facing backwards even though the night before the employees straightened everything up. When the park's security are making their nightly patrols, some officers have witnessed a man peering out from different windows, watching their every move. When they enter the studio to check for trespassers, the building is always empty of anything living.

One evening, Craig, a Grand Canyon Association employee, was closing up the building alone. He had done a sweep earlier in the downstairs theater area to make sure all the visitors had departed. While he was upstairs cleaning, Craig distinctly heard footsteps on the creaky staircase that lead down into the theater's room. Thinking he must have accidentally overlooked a guest in the building, Craig walked over towards the downstairs door and called out, "I'm sorry folks, we're closed. You are going to have to come back tomorrow." When Craig didn't receive a response from anyone, he became annoyed because now he had to go back downstairs and search for the trespasser. Before he started heading down the stairs, he heard a gruff man's muffled voice from the farthest back portion of the theater. When he reached the bottom of the stairs, he looked everywhere for the intruder but never found a living soul. He departed the theater in record time, grabbed his keys, and left the building.

Another employee, Brent, was opening up the Kolb Studio one morning. Brent went downstairs into the theater room to make sure everything was up and running. He heard someone walking on the staircase and looked up to see who had arrived. Hovering on the staircase was a black mass in the shape of a human. He said it was just floating about a foot above the stairs and he knew it was watching him. Before his eyes, the being slowly dissipated into thin air. He didn't have to be told twice to get the hell out of the basement. No one knows just who is haunting Kolb Studio, but if you enter into this building, show some respect just in case its Emery or Ellsworth Kolb making sure their home is being well cared for.

Chapter 12
COLTER HALL

In the early twentieth century, visits to the Grand Canyon were growing in popularity. It was quickly determined that more employees were needed for the spike in tourism. The major dilemma became where would they house all the new employees. Once again, Mary Colter was called in for her assistance in designing two separate dormitories, one for single women only (Colter Hall) and the other being for single men (Victor Hall). These buildings would become the last two projects in the Grand Canyon Village that Mary Colter would be contracted to design. Both buildings were constructed with the help of local native stones.

Completed in 1937, this dorm became the temporary home for female employees (Harvey Girls) working for the Fred Harvey Company. This building has multiple floors at different levels with seventy-five sleeping quarters. Each room contains two beds, a couple of dressers, an extremely small closet, a window, and a sink and mirror. There is a common room where female employees can watch television, socialize, and cook a meal. Several large shared bathrooms are located towards the middle of each main floor. Showering can be difficult because there is only four shower stalls on each floor and they have to be shared with roughly one hundred and fifty women. Living in such close proximity to each other can at times become frustrating, plus the thin walls between rooms can make women seeking out peace and quiet nearly impossible. No men are allowed inside the building after 8 p.m., and quiet hours begin at 10 p.m. However, these rules are loosely enforced by security. Located on Village Loop Drive, it's an easy walk for employees from the Bright Angel Lodge and El Tovar Hotel to get to work, plus it is conveniently located almost directly on the rim but just far enough away that the noise from all the visitors won't disturb anyone. In the summertime, this dorm becomes the home of seasonal employees traveling from different countries. It is truly a unique experience to meet people from all sorts of different backgrounds and cultures.

There is even a local legend that there is an underground tunnel that leads directly from Colter to Victor Hall. This tunnel is also rumored to be haunted, however, these rumors have never been investigated and this chapter is only about the dormitories, so, let's get into all the spooky stuff, shall we?

Colter Hall has continuously housed women of all ages since it first opened with many of these ladies staying for multiple years. With that said, it should come as no surprise that women have passed away within the walls of this building from sickness and old age and unfortunately suicides. There have also been female employees that lived in Colter Hall who have accidently fallen to their deaths off the rim or succumbed to accidents within the park's boundaries. Well, let me be honest about this old, grim structure. This is one of the most haunted buildings I have ever lived in, let alone been too. Many women living here have heard, seen, and felt things that cannot be explain away, and walking the halls alone at night or just being alone in your room ... well, this building just seems to manifest creepy vibes.

If Walls Could Talk

Annie was offered a job working at the Bright Angel Lodge in May 2013. When she arrived at the canyon, Annie went directly to the Human Resources' building to fill out paperwork and get drug tested. When she completed all the processes to become a park employee, she was sent to the Housing Department to receive her bedding and be assigned a room that included a roommate. Annie choose room 14, which is located on the first floor. After she received the key to her new room, Annie was driven to Colter Hall with a few personal belongings that she brought with her to the canyon. She walked around the dreary hallways until she was finally able to located her room. When she entered the room, she saw two small twin beds, a dresser for her personal possessions, and one immensely tiny closet that she had to share with a total stranger. The only thing missing from the room was her new roommate. A couple hours later, as Annie was resting on her bed, the door opened and in walked Lindsey, her new roommate.

Annie and Lindsey hit it off from the beginning and became good friends. Both women worked in different areas of the park and rarely saw each other. Annie found herself alone in the room more often then she cared for and the whole Colter Hall structure just seemed sinister. One evening while Annie was reading, she heard someone running and laughing up and down the halls outside of her room. After it happened a couple more times, Annie became annoyed, got off her bed, and opened up the door to her room, leading into the hallway to ask the people if they could be a little quieter. As she flung the door open, she was surprised to see that no one was there. That was impossible, because right outside her door was a small staircase leading up to the main hallway, so the person or persons could not have vanished so quickly. Mystified, she shut the door and returned back to her bed to continue reading. Around thirty seconds later, Annie clearly heard loud thumping again coming from the hallway as if someone was running and jumping around. She flew off the bed and threw the door open to have words with the person, but once again, no one was there.

When Lindsey finally came home from work that night, Annie tried to tell her about the strange experience. But Lindsey, a full-blown skeptic of the paranormal, tried to come up with some off-the-wall explanation for what Annie thought she heard. Not wanting to get into an argument with her new friend, Lindsey cut the conversation short and the two women retired for the night.

The next day when Annie arrived at work, she started asking her co-workers if anyone knew if Colter Hall was haunted. Several women that live in the building said that they totally believe that something supernatural reside within its walls. Some women claimed to have had unexplainable things happen to them while others say they have known residents in the dormitory that have claimed to have witnessed full-bodied apparitions. About three weeks after Annie arrived at the park, the housing dept was going to relocate her to a room in Trailer Village. The night before she left, Annie was lying on her bed reading and her roommate Lindsey was sitting on her bed with headphones on, listening to music playing from her laptop. As both girls were in their own little worlds, a strange scratching sound began at their rooms only window. Annie didn't think much of it at first, believing a branch from a nearby tree was brushing up against the window, but then the scratching became so loud and irritating that Annie wasn't able to concentrate on what she was reading. She set her book down and walked over to the window to see what was creating the nails-on-blackboard sound. She was not able see anyone or anything that could be making the sound, though she did notice that there was a slight breeze blowing outside.

Annie, however, did not believe that this sound was being created by anything paranormal. Not having been able to detect what was making the sound and since it seemed to have stopped, she went back to her bed to continue reading. Within a few minutes, the scratching sound resumed, but louder as if someone was trying to get the girls attention. This time, Lindsey had heard the scratching sounds, which over-powered the music on her headphones. The two roomies eyes met and Lindsey said, "What the hell was that?" Annie replied that something had been scratching at the window for a few minutes. They both got off their beds and walked over to the window to look out and see what was making the horrendous sound. There were no tree branches anywhere near the window and they couldn't see anybody walking around outside, it should also be noted that it had snowed earlier in the day and there was no tracks of any footprints in the freshly fallen snow.

Annie walked back to her bed, picked up her book and continued to read, while Lindsey went back to her computer, but avoided putting her headphones back on so if the sound came back, she could hear it. A few minutes later, the mirror above their sink slowly opened, exposing the medicine cabinet inside. Annie once again got out of her bed, walked over to the mirror, and closed it. As Annie returned to her bed for the third time, Lindsey blurted out that old buildings tend to make strange noises. A little while had passed and both girls had almost forgotten about the strange things happening within their room, when all of a sudden the mirror flew violently open and the cold water at the sink turned on by itself at full blast. This paranormal episode left Lindsey finally without any words. Annie could hardly wait for the next day when she would be moving out of Colter Hall. After she was relocated to Trailer Village, she refused to ever step foot back inside this old creepy building.

What's Living in the Closet?

Carrie began working at the Grand Canyon in 2014. Having recently gone through a bitter divorce, Carrie thought that finding a job at the Grand Canyon would help with healing her broken heart. She loves to hike, photograph animals, stargaze, and just be one with nature. Now that Carrie was single, Colter Hall would become her new home. She was assigned to room 54, which is located on the second floor. Carrie fell in love with her new surroundings and made new friends quickly. One evening while she was watching a movie on her laptop computer and lying in bed, she thought she heard something inside her closet. She got off the bed, walked over to the closet door, and opened it. Nothing seemed out of the ordinary, but she decided to look around to see if a rodent had nested inside the closet and might be the reason for the noise. Carrie rummaged through boxes, shoes, and clothing, but was unable to find any living creature inside the closet. Satisfied that no wild animal or icky rodent had taken up residency in her room, Carrie closed the closet door and turned to go back to her bed, when it sounded as if someone punched the inside of the closet door. Carrie claimed that she hadn't been that scared since she accidentally stumbled across a black bear while back-packing through Glacier National Park in Montana. Carrie tried to convince herself that she just didn't place one of the boxes in the closet back securely on the top shelf and it fell on the door. The last thing she wanted to do was clean up any mess. She slowly went back towards the closet and cautiously opened the door in case the box's lid came off and spilled out its contents. As the door opened just far enough for her to be able to peek inside to see what had fallen, she was surprised to see that once again everything was in its proper place. Carrie knew the walls in Colter Hall were paper thin and now assumed that she was hearing her neighbors in the next room.

The next day, Carrie felt that she needed to speak to her neighbors and ask them if they could please keep the noise down. She knocked on their door and when they opened it Carrie politely told them that the noise coming from their room the night before was just a little too loud. Both of the girls seemed confused and told her that they had also heard some weird pounding sounds all night coming from within their closet, and they thought Carrie and her roommate were the cause of the commotion. Carrie couldn't believe what she was hearing and explained to them that her roommate was on vacation and had not been in the park for at least a week. The three girls sat down and discussed what they had all experienced the night before which was very similar in nature. Later that same evening, Carrie was once again watching a movie on her laptop when pounding sounds began to come from her closet once again. As she sat up in bed staring at her closet door, knocking also began on the front door. Carrie didn't know what to do when until she distinctly heard her neighbors voices calling out to her from outside of the front door telling her to open up.

Both girls were also experiencing strange sounds coming from their closet too. Carrie quickly invited the girls into her room and were able to witness the same strange sounds emanating from her closet as well. All three girls decided that until Carrie's roommate came back from her vacation, Carrie could sleep with them in their room.

The sleeping arrangements were simple, the two neighbor girls would share a bed and Carrie would have a bed to herself. The next night as the girls were sleeping, Carrie was startled awake by something violently grabbing one of her legs and yanking her off the bed onto the floor, which awoke the other two girls. The two terrified neighbors jumped off their bed and ran over to see what happened and to see if Carrie was injured. After this last incident, Carrie knew that the two rooms were haunted by something malevolent. While the two girls were trying to console Carrie, their voices were overpowered by a sound that resembled many plastic bags being rustled at the same time, and then a loud bang for the finishing touch. The next day, Carrie began to look for a new room to live in. She thoroughly believes Colter Hall is a portal to the undead.

I'll Miss You When You're Gone

Molly had been living at Colter Hall for a few years and had lived in several different rooms during her stay here. The last room she lived in was room 65, which is on the second floor. Molly knew about all the ghosts that residents claim they have encountered inside this buildings dismal hallways and rooms. Molly also has stated that she too has had several paranormal experiences during her stay, but on her last night within this old dormitory, she and her overnight guest were both entertained by what they believed to be a ghost. Molly had found love at the canyon and was soon married to another park employee. The housing department tries its best to accommodate married couples, however housing can be sparse during certain times of the year, which means couples may be placed on a waiting list until a room becomes available. Molly and her new husband had finally received the call that a room had become vacant and they were going to be relocated to a coed dormitory near Trailer Village. Molly had decided that on her last night in Colter Hall, she was going to sneak her new husband into her room to spend the night with her. The newlyweds were cuddled up on the small twin bed talking about their future life together when a beautiful bluish mist came out of the ceiling and gradually descended upon them until it was within a couple of feet of them, then it just hovered. Molly and her husband watched this mist in amazement for about two minutes before it drifted back up towards the ceiling and disappeared. Immediately, the married couple knew that they had just witnessed one of Colter Hall's many spirits and Molly believes to this day that this was Colter Halls way of telling her "Goodbye."

Chapter 13

VICTOR HALL

Victor Hall was constructed in 1936 as the male-only dormitory just one year before Colter Hall was finished. The overall design was more practical than elegant compared to other Mary Colter buildings, although it was still built to Colter's strict design standards, with native rock, brown wood siding, and green window trim, it tends to blend in with the natural woodland surroundings. Being adjacent to the canyon's train tracks, this dorm isn't situated in the best location if you were looking for privacy and silent nights. The location was also chosen so that paying overnight guests wouldn't be bothered by the off-duty park male employees. Another reason for the location was to keep the single males away from the single females while off the clock.

This old historic building has since been infamously nicknamed by village locals as "Victim Hall." It has been the gruesome site of many drunken brawls, physical and sexual assaults, thefts, vandalisms, and even murders. Wild parties are constantly broken up by park rangers and occasionally trouble makers are arrested and even banned from re-entering the park. Yes, the Grand Canyon Village comes equipped with a jail, court house, and a strict judge. With all of the negative energy associated with this dorm, there is understandably quite a few alarming stories that have been known to keep some residents awake at night.

Quite a few of the male residents have encountered a malevolent spirit that has been known to enter their rooms at night and strangle them as they sleep, while pinning them to their beds. Many unsuspecting men have also been violently pushed around by an unseen force as they are strolling around through the aging halls and corridors. New employees have never heard about any of the paranormal activity that occurs within this building walls, so the newbies have no idea what they are walking into. Just looking at this building from the outside should give even the bravest guy the shivers.

You're Never Alone

New park employee Daniel was hired as a seasonal employee for the summer season of 2014. Daniel was nineteen years old at the time of his hire and was from Thailand. In his homeland, Daniel told me that his family's personal belief about the supernatural is that spirits are evil and are only on earth to cause harm to the living. He had considered himself lucky that during his lifetime, he had never come face to face with a ghost. One night after work, Daniel stopped by his dorm room to grab his personal hygiene items and a towel so he could take a shower, which was located down the hallway. The washroom door is normally propped open. After he finished his shower, Daniel walked towards the bathroom's large mirror so he could shave and brush his teeth. As he was putting toothpaste onto his toothbrush, he swore that out of his peripheral vision he could see someone standing in the hallway watching him. He quickly turned his head to see who it was, but no one was there. Thinking he must have imagined it, Daniel shrugged it off and continued brushing his teeth. When he finished up inside the bathroom and gathered his belongings, he started to head towards the door leading into the hallway when he stopped dead in his tracks as he saw an extremely tall, black, featureless figure hovering in the hallway watching him. To his horror, this phantom began to glide towards him. Unable to breath or move, Daniel closed his eyes and prayed for it to go away. After what felt like an eternity, he slowly opened his eyes and the entity was gone. Daniel was traumatized about what he saw and could hardly wait for his time to end at the canyon so he could return home.

On the first floor there is a malicious entity that likes to torment men while they sleep. Well into the darkness of the night, after most of the residents inside Victor Hall have decided to get some shuteye, an angry male spirit has been known to stand at the end of unsuspecting victims' beds and violently shake their mattress or rip their blankets off of them. Witnesses who have actually claimed to have seen this malevolent entity have stated that its face is pure evil and they could feel that it wanted to cause them harm, and when it fades away it leaves a horrid scent that is reminiscent of rotten eggs. Another terrifying experience residents of Victor Hall have claimed to have had is that while they are sleeping, something powerful will physically restrain them on their beds. Other men have stated that as they were struggling to break free from the entities grasp, it seemed to anger the wraith even more and it would forcefully throw them off of their bed onto the floor. One man that was living in a room by himself said that he ended up receiving a bloody lip from his encounter with this spirit.

When Things Go Bump in the Night

When autumn arrives at the Grand Canyon, most of the seasonal employees have returned from where they came and the park operates with a bare minimum of staff members to get by for the winter season. Year-round employees love this time of year because they normally don't have to share their dorm rooms with anyone else and most of the loud partying has come to an end. Gene had been employed at the park for years and was ecstatic about finally having a room all to himself. Like most longtime residents of the Grand Canyon's Village, Gene had heard more than once about all the ghost stories circulating around about Victor Hall, however he had lived in this building for many years and not once did he ever experience anything out of the ordinary—nor did he know of anyone personally who claimed to have seen a ghost. In January of 2014, Gene's work schedule for the next day was going to start earlier than normal so not having a roommate to keep him awake, he decided to go to bed early.

Gene had been asleep for about three hours when a thundering boom came from the direction of his closet and abruptly awoke him from a deathlike sleep. As he sat up, he looked at the time on his clock and it read 2:48 a.m. He figured the guy living in the room next to his must have dropped something, so he laid back down and tried to go back to sleep. A few minutes later another loud thud once again came from his closet. Gene angrily jumped out of bed, opened the closet door, and began pounded on the wall leading to his neighbor's room, hollering for him to stop making noise. When he thought the guy next door got the message, he stumbled back into bed, rolled over, and faced the wall. As he began to doze off, Gene heard someone walking around in his room.

At first he was too frightened to move, but when he heard the footsteps stop right next to his bed, Gene knew he had to protect himself in any way possible. But as he began to turn to confront the intruder, he realized he couldn't move a muscle and was somehow being physically restrained to his bed by something powerful. Gene finally managed to turn his head to see who was restraining him and couldn't believe his eyes. There was no one that he could physically see in his room, let alone next to his bed. As if to punish Gene for turning his head, whatever was pinning him down began to physically punch Gene, which was accompanied with a terrifying non-human growl. His ghostly assailant finally stopped after Gene felt a blow to his mouth that made him taste blood. Just as quickly as it started, it was over. Gene fought to untangle himself from his blankets, and when he finally broke free he flipped the light on as quickly as possible. He searched every inch of the room, looking for anything that might give him a clue as to what had just happened to him. He could still taste blood so he walked over to a mirror where he saw that his lip was split from where he was punched. Gene realized that no living person had come into his room. He now believes the stories that "Victim Hall" is haunted by an evil entity.

Chapter 14

HAUNTINGS
ARE EVERYWHERE

As you can see from the previous chapters, the Grand Canyon Village has more than its fair share of hauntings in its lodges, restaurants, gift stores, campgrounds, and hiking trails. However, the village is much larger than most visitors realize. There is a medical center, different business offices for the different companies that work inside the park, bus stops, an auto shop, a recreational facility for park employees, and actual family housing. These areas also contain paranormal activity, and some of it is downright terrifying for anyone unlucky enough to come into contact with the malicious specters.

Bus Stop Adjacent to El Tovar

The Grand Canyon shuttle buses are possibly the best way to travel within the very busy village area, especially during the summer season. There are fourteen shuttle stops that begin at the Grand Canyon's main Visitors Center. The shuttles make a loop around the Grand Canyon Village and the stops are located at popular tourist destinations and lodges. It's a fifty-minute round-trip ride if you remain on the bus, which eventually ends up back at the Grand Canyon Visitor Center where you began your trip. If you decide to take the shuttle into the village from the Visitor Center (which is highly recommended), the third shuttle stop will put you at the sidewalk leading to the El Tovar Hotel and directly across from the historic Grand Canyon Depot. Nothing seems out of the ordinary here during the daytime hours, but as you sit at the shuttle stop after the sun goes down … well, that's a whole different story. Many tourists and employees have felt an evil presence as you sit waiting for the shuttle. People have heard their names being called from across the street towards the Railroad Depot. One female tourist claimed she was sitting alone at the bus stop one night and felt something caress her arm. Some other witnesses have claimed that they could clearly hear as if someone was breathing into their ear when they were alone. This shuttle stop gives a new meaning to terror.

General Office Building

The General Office building, which sits just to the left of the Grand Canyons Public Library, is where park concessionaire Xanterra operates from. To the rear of this structure is the only auto shop within the borders of Grand Canyon National Park. When the village was first established, the original Grand Canyon mule barn was housed where Xanterra's general office building now sits. As the years passed, a more suitable location was established to board the mules. The old barn was conveniently located at the crossroads leading to the El Tovar Hotel and Hopi House, so the Fred Harvey Company (Xanterra) turned this spot into their General Office building. Paranormal happenings on this property have frightened many employees. The women's restroom (only for employees) has a paper towel dispenser that comes equipped with a motion activated sensor.

This holder automatically disperses enough paper towels to dry your hands. Well, it was a good idea, but unfortunately a playful ghost likes to frequent the women's restroom and empty out the paper towel holder. In the early mornings when the first female employee walks into the restroom, they may find a pile of paper towels in a heap on the floor. This seems to be a favorite past time for the ghost. Workers also hear their names being called by disembodied voices. This wouldn't have been very frightening if they weren't the only person left inside the building at night. Shadow figures have also been seen walking through the hallway, and a few late-night employees will abruptly decide it is time to go home when they see these shadows pass by their open doors.

Grand Canyon Auto Services (which helps customers with belts, batteries, tires, fuses etc.) has a playful ghost that likes to hide the mechanics' hand tools from time to time. Also, on some mornings when the shop opens, car parts that the technicians had been working on the night before will found in different areas around the shop, making grumpy mechanics even grumpier. One mechanic has even claimed to have witnessed a full-bodied male apparition wearing clothing from the 1930s era with a brown cowboy hat walk through the garage and then disappeared into thin air. Old timers have claimed that when the General Office building was still the park's mule barn, a man was murdered on the property. I wasn't able to find any proof of this crime, but it's possible because the park didn't keep accurate record of any deaths within the park until after 1974.

Engineering Building

The Engineering Building is a large metal structure that lies south of the railroad tracks across from the Bright Angel Lodge. Nothing out of the ordinary seems to happen here during the daytime, but as soon after the sun sets, this property harbors an evil force. One evening in 2013, at around 2:00 a.m., a security officer was making his nightly rounds. He decided to pull into the parking area next to the building to fill out some paperwork. While he was sitting in his vehicle updating his nightly forms, he saw a large herd of deer walk between his car and the dreary complex and begin to graze on some plants. A little while later, the officer glanced up towards the deer and noticed that the herd was transfixed on watching something climbing up the outside staircase attached to building. The officer knew that no employee was working at that time of night and he would have noticed if someone had walked up. He watched the figure for a few second and then realized he was actually witnessing something not of this world. The figure was dressed all in black and seemed to be gliding up the stairs.

The officer began to believe that what he was witnessing was just a figment of his imagination, so he looked back at the deer to see if they were still sensing something and every deer in the herd seemed as if they were under a spell and unable to look away from the specter. As soon as the figure reached the top of the staircase, it floated through a closed door and disappeared. This perplexed officer was trying to make sense of what he just observed but he still had a job to do which meant he needed to investigate to see if this was actually a real person trespassing on private property. He grabbed his large Mag-Lite, opened the door, stepped out of his patrol car, and walked over to the staircase. Once the herd saw that he was coming towards them, they ran off (however, these animals will hang out if there is a creepy ghost gliding around, go figure).

As he slowly climbed the rickety staircase, this officer didn't have to go too far up to see that the door at the top of the stairs had a locked deadbolt on it. He ran back to his patrol car and got the hell out of there. This incident wasn't included with his nightly report, because honestly, he didn't want to become the laughing stock of the department. To this day, he still has no clue what the thing climbing the stairs was; what he did know was that it wasn't of flesh or blood.

Lodge and restaurant employees that work the evening shifts choose to walk home if they don't want to wait forty-five minutes for the employee shuttle to pick them up. Victor Hall residents and other park employees lucky enough to live in the actual single-family housing section (managers, assistant managers, and leads) usually prefer to walk home if their jobs are in the main village area. There is a shortcut most locals know about that heads towards Victor Hall and the family housing area that takes the person across the railroad tracks and next to the engineering structure. One evening, Monica, a lead at the Bright Angel Lodge decided, she would rather take the shortcut home since it was going to be over a half hour wait until the employee shuttle would return. Monica crossed over the railroad tracks, and as she had almost completely passed by the engineering property, someone grabbed her throat from behind and started to strangle her. She was struggling desperately to break free from whoever was trying to harm her, yet she couldn't feel any flesh or bones as she was flailing around. Just as Monica felt as though she was about to pass out, the pressure around her throat came to an end. Falling to her knees, she took in a deep breath, then looked to see who her assailant was.

There was no one anywhere in sight and it was impossible for anyone to have fled so quickly do to the open area. Then she realized that she had never heard any footsteps approach or leave her. As soon as she returned home, she went into the bathroom where she sported a large red mark around her neck where it was grabbed. Monica has refused to ever take the shortcut home again if it was dark out.

Monica has said that she has heard about other people having eerie encounters around the Engineering Building but never took the stories seriously. When she told me about her frightening assault, I was skeptical at first and thought that maybe she was making the whole thing up, until another employee insisted on talking to me about a horrifying encounter he also had endured near the exact same spot where Monica's assault occurred.

A couple of weeks after Monica's terrifying encounter, Richard, who was a server at the Arizona Room Restaurant, was also taking the shortcut home to Victor Hall after a long and busy night at work. Richard was also passing the Engineering Building when he was grabbed from behind and violently thrown to the ground by something that possessed superhuman strength. After Richard was able to get his thoughts together, he quickly jumped to his feet to face his assailant. This Arizona Room server is not a small guy and can hold his own in a fight, which he thought was going to happen until he realized that he was all alone. This was puzzling because there was no place that the other party could have run to without having been seen. Richard didn't want to hang around, so as he turned to start walking home, once again something from behind him shoved him so hard that his feet left the ground. When Richard hit the ground, he thought his right wrist had broken in the fall, plus he suffered from multiple abrasions. Trying to gather what energy he had left, Richard finally got to his feet, turned to see who was tormenting him, and once again he was all alone. Richard ran from that area as fast as he could. Several people have claimed to have been assaulted by an unseen presence near or around this building. My advice: find a different way home.

Building A

Building A is located at the bottom of the road that heads up to the El Tovar Hotel and the Hopi House. This multilevel structure was constructed using native rock and is set back into the hillside. Building A houses the offices to some of the top officials for the Xanterra Company plus one of the parks lost and found centers. Walking or driving by this rustic yet charming site during the daylight hours gives sightseers a deceptively pleasant view, but as soon as the sun begins to set, look out. Building A is one of the sites that the park's nighttime security staff will actually walk through to make sure everything is safe and secure. While some of these officers have never admitted to having encountered anything out of normal within its walls, there are a select few who dread having to patrol its interior. A few officers have reported hearing disembodied footsteps following them through the building, the sound of something pounding on the walls, doors slamming shut, and disembodied voices. Even during the daylight hours, a few employees have been known to leave early because they also hear things that can't be explained away.

The Manager's House

When park managers Karen and Katrina were offered an actual home in the residential district, they were both overly ecstatic. Being offered your own home that you don't have to share with anybody else while being employed at the canyon is like winning the lottery. Both women had been exceptional and dedicated employees and they were finally rewarded by being given their own home within the Grand Canyon National Park. The couple had learned that the former tenants had quickly up and left the house and decided to relocate to a small duplex, which didn't make a lot of sense because they had heard that this family had children, and the house they abandoned was perfect for a family.

After Karen and Katrina settled in, they began unpacking their belongings and tried to figure out the best locations around their new home to place their furnishings. It took a couple of weeks to empty all of their boxes and now the house had become a home. Karen was home alone one day, resting, when she thought she heard a little girl talking from one of the bedrooms. Thinking that maybe one of her new neighbors had children playing outside, she just assumed the voice was reverberating through her new home. Later that night after Karen and Katrina had gone to bed, they were both awaken by the same little girl's voice that Karen had heard earlier in the day. They couldn't believe that a parent would allow their child to be outside at such a late hour in the night, but what confused them even more about hearing this voice was that all the windows in their home was closed and locked.

The next morning when Karen and Katrina were headed towards their car to go to work, they were finally able to meet their next-door neighbor. Karen didn't see any children in their car, so she slyly asked what the ages were of their children. The male neighbor seemed a little embarrassed and said that he and his wife didn't have any kids. Before he got in his car, he looked at the couple and asked them why they assumed he had any children. Karen didn't know what to say so she told him that they were just trying to make conversation. He smiled at the two women before driving away.

Karen and Katrina knew that they had heard a little girl talking inside their home and were now more intrigued than before. As days passed into weeks, they both noticed that things around the house would disappear only to reappear at a later time, but never in the same place it had previously been. One of the bedrooms would always be unnaturally cold, even during the warm summer months. Karen was finally able to locate the previous family that had resided in the house before her and asked them if they had ever experienced anything strange when they lived there. The woman that had lived in the house was Cindy. She didn't really want to talk to anyone about her time living there. Karen tried to break the ice by telling Cindy about strange occurrences happening to her and Katrina and about hearing a little girl talking, but that she can never find the source of the voice. It took Cindy a couple of minutes listening to Karen's stories when she finally opened up and told the story about why they before the house so quickly.

Cindy and her husband have one child, a daughter named Taylor, and she was only five years old. After they moved into the house, Cindy would hear Taylor alone in her bedroom talking to someone that she just assumed was her daughter's dolls. One day while cleaning, Cindy heard her daughter seemingly having a conversation with someone else, so she decided to walk into Taylor's bedroom and ask her who she was talking to. Taylor excitedly told her mother that she was talking with her friend Emma. Cindy thought her daughter must have an imaginary friend. After a while, Cindy began to notice that her daughter was becoming withdrawn and only wanted to stay in her bedroom to play with her friend Emma. One early morning, Cindy went into Taylor's bedroom to wake her up and get her dressed so they could take a trip into Flagstaff. Taylor wasn't in her room, so Cindy started searching the house with no luck of finding her little girl. Cindy glanced out of the living room window and saw Taylor sitting in the middle of the street. This petrified mother ran outside to the street and pulled Taylor to safety. Cindy scolded her daughter, reminded her about them telling her over and over again that streets are dangerous, and demanded that she say why she disobeyed the rules by: number one, going outside without any supervision, and number two, playing in the street. Taylor looked up at her mom and said, "Emma told me that if I played in the street, we could be together forever." That was the last day they lived in the house.

This confirmed Karen's suspicion that she was living in a haunted house. To this day, things still go missing and she still hears a little girl's voice talking every now and then around the house. Karen and Katrina have refused to move, and they consider this ghost child as family.

CONCLUSION

Grand Canyon National Park is among the most beautiful places on earth. Along with all this natural beauty, however, is a lot of tragedy. Death occurs here somewhat frequently. There are so many other stories to be told and still some that have yet to be discovered. The primary purpose of this book is to give the general public the knowledge that the Grand Canyon Village is infested with ghosts and hauntings and that the majority of these stories have never been told. I personally became tired and bored from reading the same old ghost stories told and retold over and over again. My husband and I found that many authors who write on the paranormal seem to just talk about the same, overwritten-about, haunted locations. I want readers to know that there are thousands of haunted places around the world that receive no attention. The Grand Canyon takes up a large area of land in Northern Arizona and we will never know all the accurate history that has happened in this giant abyss. The Grand Canyon National Park as a whole contains more paranormal activity than any location I have ever been to or read about. I have been actively involved with the paranormal since I was a toddler and I have lived in many haunted houses throughout my life. All the stories in this book are true, and I hope the reader felt a chill down go down their spine … or was it one of the many ghosts that call the Grand Canyon home?

BIBLIOGRAPHY

Berger, Todd. *It Happened at the Grand Canyon*. Kearney, NE: Morris Book Publishing, 2007.

Ghiglier, Michael P. and Thomas M. Myers. *Over the Edge: Death in Grand Canyon*. Puma Press, 2012.

Hefley, Flood. *Grand Canyon Trivia Trek: An Intrepid Rim-to-Rim Historical Journey*. Boulder, CO: Big Earth Publishing, 2012.

Kaiser, James. *Grand Canyon: The Complete Guide*. Destination Press, 2011.

Lago, Don. *Grand Canyon Trivia*. Helena, MT: Riverbend Publishing, 2009.

Neuner, John D. *Arizona Myths, Fallacies, and Misconceptions*. First Leaf Publisher, 2001.

Trimble, Marshall. *Roadside History of Arizona*. Missoula, MT: Mountain Press Publishing, 1986.

Additional Resources

Arizona State Library, Archives, and Public Records. "Arizona's Chronology." https://azlibrary.gov/arizona-almanac/arizonas-chronology

Burnett, Jim. "Longest-Running Film in History Highlighted in New Park Exhibit." December 23, 2011. https://www.nationalparkstraveler.org/2011/12/longest-running-film-history-highlighted-new-park-exhibit9188

Campbell, Mike. "The Hance Guestbook: In praise of John Hance and his tall tales." April 15, 2015. https://www.canyonology.com/hance-guestbook-praise-john-hance-tall-tales/

History.com. "Arizona." https://www.history.com/topics/us-states/arizona

Legends of America. www.legendsofamerica.com

National Park Service. "Grand Canyon." http://www.nps.gov/grca//index.htm

Native Languages of the Americas. www.native-language.org

Nature, History and Culture at the Grand Canyon (NHCGC). http://grcahistory.org

Suran, William C. "With the Wings of an Angel: A Biography of Ellsworth and Emery Kolb." 1991. http://www.grandcanyonhistory.org/Publications/Kolb/kolb.html

To Write the Author

If you wish to contact the author or would like more information about this book, please write to the author in care of Llewellyn Worldwide, and we will forward your request. Both the author and publisher appreciate hearing from you and learning of your enjoyment of this book and how it has helped you. Llewellyn Worldwide cannot guarantee that every letter written to the author can be answered, but all will be forwarded. Please write to:

Brian-James Martinez and Judy Martinez
⁒ Llewellyn Worldwide
2143 Wooddale Drive
Woodbury, MN 55125.2989

Please enclose a self-addressed stamped envelope for reply,
or $1.00 to cover costs. If outside the U.S.A., enclose
an international postal reply coupon.